GRAPPLING WITH GRIEF

GRAPPLING WITH GRIEF

A guide for the bereaved

Penny Rawson

KARNAC

LONDON   NEW YORK

First published in 2005 by
H. Karnac (Books) Ltd.
6 Pembroke Buildings, London NW10 6RE

British Library Cataloguing in Publication Data

A C.I.P. for this book is available from the British Library

  ISBN 1 85575 321 9

Edited, designed and produced by The Studio Publishing Services Ltd, Exeter EX4 8JN

Printed by Hobbs the Printers Ltd, Southampton

10 9 8 7 6 5 4 3 2 1

www.karnacbooks.com

CONTENTS

ACKNOWLEDGEMENTS

This book was inspired by a dream that Terry Halifax related to me some time after the death of his late wife Agnes. So many people are affected seriously by grief and are unaware of what is happening to them. I am grateful to the many people who have shared their experiences of grief with me in my role as counsellor/therapist. I have drawn from this experience but all the clinical examples have pseudonyms and some are fictitional, based on an amalgamation of several clients' stories.

I would like to thank those who have been kind enough to read and comment upon the early drafts of this book and whose encouraging comments have kept me going. These include Sheila Short and Marjorie Garwell, Catherine Swan, Joyce Shepherd-Thorne, Maureen Halifax, and especially Shirley Crofts, Father Tom, and Terry Halifax, who kindly read and proof-read more than one draft.

Thanks too to Karnac for agreeing to publish this, my second book.

This book is dedicated to those who have taught me about bereavement either indirectly or directly. Especially the following: Moira, Donal, Margot, Mary, Eileen, Joss, Eileen, Basil, Eric, Kathleen, Peta, Paul, Father Kahle, Bobby, Arthur, Kathleen, Carola, Susan, Maria, Louis, Agnes, Barbara, Avril, Frances and Giza.

FOREWORD

About one hundred years ago Francis Thompson, the poet and essayist, wrote:

> To be understood—that is the noble travail of all men: except some noble few who would yet more gladly receive and understand. To attain both is the most soaring of human ambitions: to attain either the most seldom compassed of human experiences. We move—all of us—under disguises, the rending of which would leave life intolerable, the presence of which makes life a doubt.

He fled into opium and alcohol as his disguise and to help him cope.

This book gives the readers the sense that they are being understood and helped to understand themselves and others as they grieve.

In the following pages Dr Rawson reveals herself as an experienced psychotherapist and as a woman, and draws on both sets of experiences in a very clear way, using language and images with which most of us can feel at home.

To do this is to trust her readers to "tread gently on her dreams". She quotes from people with whom, as her clients, she walked through precious and delicate times. She also quotes from a number of colleagues and friends whose words helped her in her own periods of acute sensitivity and personal grief.

In reading these pages I found reassurance as I go now into a new phase of my own life and have to leave much that I hold dear behind me. Because of the expertise hidden behind these pages, an expertise that comes out of Dr Rawson's lived and felt experience, I am sure that many others will find the way this book unfolds a great help in enabling them to disclose some of their secrets to themselves and find a way of living at ease with the truth of the new experiences that they too now have to face, to enjoy, and to live afresh with those they have loved and still love.

Brother Thomas More Mann OFM Cap
Franciscan Friary, Erith
August, 2004

Introduction

Loss is not just about a death

L oss and its consequences beset most of us at one time or another. Grief, the feeling engendered by loss, is most often associated with the loss of a loved one, but it encompasses other losses too. It might be the loss of a way of life, a relationship, a job, country, home, or physical abilities, to name but few. The way one suffers the loss will have an impact on the grieving process. A loss may be expected or sudden, accidental or deliberate. It may be violent or peaceful, it may be timely or untimely.

In this book I look at various aspects of the grieving process and I contend that these aspects would apply to all of the above losses. However, for simplicity's sake, I focus here on the loss of a loved one, leaving the reader to apply the principles explored to other losses as appropriate. Rather than concentrating exhaustively on grieving and mourning I present a number of reflections drawn from some thirty years of working as a therapist in a number of different settings, sharing with you some of the lessons that I have learned from being alongside others in their grief and, indeed, being with myself in my own. I hope that this approach may shed a little understanding on what may be happening to you as you grapple with grief. I do not claim that my observations have the rigour of academic research; they are but musings informed by years of practice, much training, and reflection.

It is perhaps helpful, therefore, to give the reader some idea of my background, so I am giving a brief outline of my professional path here.

I have long been in the field of therapy. My interest began way back when I was just a child and wondered: "What makes people tick?", and "Why do people behave as they do?" This early interest became focused on the idea of coun-selling as a result of one lecture on student counselling that I attended when I was, in fact, training to become a teacher. This one idea so intrigued me that I undertook my special study on school counsellors. It seemed to me to be such a valuable concept. So many children in school need someone to talk to, whether about their struggles with growing up, things that are disturbing them at home or, indeed, things that are causing them problems within the school environ-ment. To have the opportunity to talk in confidence to an understanding outsider is really valuable, and I am delighted to see many more schools employing counsellors now.

In the process of researching to write my special study about school counsellors, I learned about the various forms of training for counselling and therapy. It must be remembered that as this was in the early 1970s the opportunities were not as wide and varied as they are nowadays. I decided that I would like to train to become a counsellor and I was fortunate in being able to pursue a number of different courses to achieve my goal. For example, I studied at the Westminster Pastoral Foundation, The Richmond Fellowship, and the

Dympna Centre, to name the chief ones. On the academic side, I studied for my first degree with the Open University and for my Doctorate at Durham University.

When I completed my training as a counsellor/therapist I was once again fortunate and was appointed to the post of my dreams—that of College Counsellor. I enjoyed this very much for some fourteen years. Over the years I have run many therapy groups and worked with a large number of different nationalities and age groups. During one year I counted fifty-two nationalities within my case load. I have managed counselling/therapy services, worked with young people and older people, in counselling centres and in private practice.

In these various settings I became more and more interested in brief psychotherapy, and undertook a research project on this subject leading to a Ph.D. at Durham University. Later, I drew on this to write my first book *Short Term Psychodynamic Psychotherapy: An Analysis of Key Principles* (2002). I have also spoken about the brief approach on Carlton Television in a *This Morning* programme called "What Therapy".

Mystery

One of the discoveries that I made, while undertaking my research work, was the aspect of mystery in the work of therapy. What happens in the course of therapy and within that very special relationship has a mystery element. It is hard to know how change occurs, or what exactly has made a difference, but something does happen within the counselling/therapy sessions that brings about change. Martin Buber describes it as a "meeting" which mysteriously leads to change.

My own strong belief in God has supported me in my work—not that I in any way believe it proper to impose my beliefs on others—and my reflections are at times clearly coloured by my faith and my belief in the importance of the spiritual.

I find that a faith and belief in a greater reality than this earthly one is a great comfort, a way of making sense of death and, indeed, life. I mention this not to put the reader off, but to alert those who are interested, that Chapter Four is devoted to these thoughts and to warn those who abhor any mention of the spiritual that perhaps that chapter is one to avoid! It is my observation, however, that, in an age of changing values and reduced church attendance, there is an upsurge in interest in the "spiritual". People are searching for a relationship with a "higher being", and for the mystical, and are attracted to various forms of meditation. This search for meaning is so often highlighted at times of loss and grief.

Why this book?

A very large percentage of the people whom I have seen for therapy, in the various settings that I have mentioned above, come with issues related to grief. I recall, in my early days of counselling and therapy, talking to a more experienced therapist who reckoned that most people came for therapy because of loss. At the time I was somewhat sceptical, but over the years I have come to appreciate why he made the comment. A very high percentage of clients do have issues around loss. Some come into the counsellor's office saying straight away that their loved one has died, and it is clear that this is what they wish to talk about. Very many others do not realize initially that loss is underneath their presenting problem, which may be anxiety or depression. They might come in saying, "Everything is going all wrong", or "I'm just not coping", or "I'm so depressed". It is only as we begin to talk together about their situation that the bereavement comes to light. When it does surface, it is very often this that becomes the focus of the counselling sessions. In exploring the issues around the loss that they have experienced, they find that, in realizing that they are grieving and addressing this, the "depression" or "anxiety" lifts. The loss may have happened recently or, as is very often the case, some time ago. Grieving is, in fact, a very human and normal process. It is necessary and good to grieve and it is not "sick" to do so. It is hard, very hard. It involves sadness and sorrow but most people find that, once they realize where the feelings that they are grappling with come from, then they are able to cope with it. Realizing that they are grieving does not negate the pain, but makes it more manageable. Coping with it sometimes includes the specialist support of a counsellor for a few sessions before they feel ready to continue their journey with the ordinary other supports in their lives. These may include family, friends, colleagues at work, leisure activities, and so on.

The need for education about grief before the loss

I have often needed to inform clients of the very varied, yet normal, reactions that people experience in the light of losses in their lives. This has led me to believe that more needs to be said about it *before* people find themselves grappling with grief and floundering around completely unprepared for the emotional upheaval that it may cause. I believe that if we were more informed, then the grieving process that will come to most of us, at some time in our lives, could be made a little easier by knowing, at least to some degree, what we might expect. Often clients will say, "This is the first person whom I have cared about who has died". This is often said almost apologetically, as if by way of explanation as to why they are finding it all so confusing. There is, of course, no need at all for such an apologetic air; indeed, I suggest that it is our educational system which should be apologetic. Why do we not receive any instruction on grief and the feelings it may engender when we are at school? Some would argue that that would be too soon, but they overlook the many children who are coping with the loss of a loved one at very early ages. The child too, especially if it is one of their parents who has died, is often left very alone in his or her grief because the surviving parent is so grief-stricken themselves that they do not necessarily take on board just how touched the child is by the whole experience. He or she will often be feeling the loss very deeply indeed.

Every loss of a loved one is hard, but it does seem that the first one we experience hits us in a rather different way. It is in the belief that it could be helpful to readers to know more about grief that has led me to write this book.

The stark reality of "death"

In looking at loss and the loss of loved ones we are in fact using euphemisms, are we not? A euphemism is defined in the *Reader's Digest Universal Dictionary* as: "The substitution of an inoffensive term for one considered offensively explicit" (1994, p. 530).

People refer to the person having "gone", "passed over", "passed away", or "passed on". We hear that they "haven't pulled through", "there was nothing more we could do", they "went peacefully". Is it easier for the one who is telling of the death, or the one who has suffered the loss, to be told in an indirect way? This often means that the person has to ask, "Are you telling me that he/she is dead?" What is it that causes the loss so often if not death, that stark reality that none can escape? Is it better to simply say, "I'm so sorry, John is dead", or is the indirect approach in some way preparing the one who has to face the loss?

"I think I'm going mad"

This chapter presents the first points I want to make about grief, in response to the statement made by so many who came to my counselling/therapy room suffering from grief but thinking that they were going mad.

Very often the sentence "I think I'm going mad" would precede a list of symptoms such as:

"I can't remember anything."

"I feel so tired . . ."

"Time seems to drag so . . . each minute feels like an hour . . ."

". . . it feels as if I'm walking through treacle."

"I keep bursting into tears . . . I go to the supermarket and pick up a can of beans and the tears flow . . .I hear a tune and the sobs start . . ."

" I can't concentrate, after a few minutes I find myself staring vacantly into space . . . not really thinking of anything and certainly not what I was trying to pay attention to."

"I don't seem to be able to make decisions—silly things, you know, like whether to have scrambled eggs or boiled eggs for breakfast. I don't know what's the matter with me."

Grief is no respecter of persons

The comments listed above are made by individuals from all walks of life. The businessman, the teacher, the student, housewife, granny, grandad, parent or child, husband or wife, partner or friend. Grief is no respecter of persons and it is grief that these people are referring to. When they walked into my office they were unaware that this was their issue, they were simply grappling with the symptoms. As they described their symptoms it would be quite clear to me that there was some kind of bereavement in their life. I would check this out with them, asking if they had had a bereavement lately, and so often I was proved right. I would then go on to wonder if they had experienced other feelings linked with grief, and as I did this they often looked both relieved and surprised. It seemed to them as though I was a mind reader. In fact I was simply seeing if they had experienced grief reactions that are very common; for example, anger.

It is usual to have feelings of anger, often seemingly irrational. You perhaps trip over the cat and feel murderous towards it, where in other circumstances the reaction would be more likely to be one of apology.

Loss of a parent

I recall Andrew, who was a young man in his twenties whose mother had just died.

Andrew took his car and drove it like crazy, far, far too fast along narrow, bendy roads. He knew it was too fast and dangerous, but was engulfed in anger that his mother had died and was beside himself with emotion. He was angry at her for leaving him, at fate, at the medical profession, at God, and at his own helplessness in being unable to prevent the death. Somehow the fast drive seemed to burn the anger away a little. Thankfully, he did not lose control of the car and all was well. He admitted, however, that had he died in the process of taking bends too fast, he would not have cared: "I knew what I was doing, I didn't care if I lived or died at that moment." It was, in fact, that concern that brought him to my counselling office. He had scared himself with his uncharacteristic reactions since he was normally a responsible driver and formerly had been enjoying life.

The loss of a parent for grown-up "children"

The loss of a parent is not to be underestimated in its effect on the grown-up children. Here I refer to men and women in their thirties, forties, and fifties. We take it for granted that young children will be very affected, but often overlook the impact on the mature "child". As Brendon, in his late fifties, said when his mother died, "I miss her so much, what a gap there is, she was my best friend."

Grief does have its norms and although people are affected to greater and lesser degrees and at different times, we humans behave fairly predictably in our reactions. I found that it was a great relief to these people to learn that they were after all *normal*. They were *not* going mad, they were simply *grieving*.

Very often, even after just one session, having now learned about grief, they were able to dispense with counselling and go on their way. Yes, still sad, still in pain, still grappling with their loss and its implications for their day-to-day lives, but seeing that grief is a normal human experience and one not requiring any further help from a counsellor.

Some will need more than just education about grief and require the continued support of a counsellor for a while. So many of us these days are living fairly solitary lives, the close-knit local families of former generations now spread far afield as we travel for work and study. Without the support of family and friends the most well balanced of us can be overcome by the strains of grief. We need support and companionship, especially at times of loss. The phone call, the letter, a visit, can all be welcome supports. I explore how we can help those who are bereaved and, indeed, how we can help ourselves, in a later chapter.

Echoes of other losses

Sometimes a new loss can become overwhelming and require the support of a professional because it has reopened an earlier loss, perhaps one that you took in your stride but that you had not fully come to terms with at the time. Perhaps at the time other concerns made you shelve your feelings and simply get on with the job. Again, this is a normal way of coping. There is no "right" way to cope. You do what you need to do.

Sometimes people do not make the connection to an earlier loss and it is only as they discuss the situation with a counsellor that it becomes apparent. Then the earlier loss also needs to be addressed in conjunction with the present one. This was so with John.

John had witnessed a workmate killed in a road accident involving road works. Several years earlier his neighbour's son was also killed in a road accident. He strongly felt that both deaths could have been avoided if better work practices were employed, but it was the second of these that "undid" him. He simply knew that he could not continue to work and was not feeling himself at all after the death, and came for counselling. After talking for some time it became apparent that this accident had triggered a lot of buried feelings and unfinished business about the earlier loss.

Multiple losses

The above example refers to a second loss some time earlier than the one that triggered the crisis, but it is not that unusual for people to have to contend with more than one death or loss of a significant other at the same time. Eileen, for example, lost her mother and one week later her father died also. To lose both parents in such a short time was utterly devastating for her. Where one parent dies, very often the remaining parent seems to "hold" aspects of the other for the children and it is only when the second parent dies that the first one is fully grieved for. It is only then that the source of knowledge about one's childhood is gone forever. The parental support is totally gone, the needing and being needed that is present in different degrees at different ages and stages of life is also gone. Once both parents are dead the "child" becomes the older generation; this can feel very odd, scary, and lonely.

Roberta lost not just two people at once but three—all of her brothers. Two died in the Falklands War and the third died in a traffic accident soon after. I referred earlier to how a young man took his car out and drove madly in his grief. Was this lad less fortunate, was it his way of grieving that led to his death? We will never know, but there is a moral here that at times of great loss perhaps one should hang up the car keys for a while or at the very least take very deliberate and special care on the roads.

Obviously Roberta's parents were also severely stressed by such a tragedy. Their daughter was now the only remaining child and they were finding it difficult to be supportive of her and, to some degree, made her feel second best as the only girl and as the only child alive. Their way of coping was to pretend the boys had never existed, destroying all evidence of them. This was intolerable for Roberta, who wanted to remember them, to mourn their passing, to talk about them, and to grapple with what their loss meant to her.

In her circumstances, where those closest to her were so lost in their own grief reaction that they could not help her, she needed to be able to talk to someone who would have time to be with her in her sorrow and mourning. She wanted someone to listen as she talked of her pain, and the things she was feeling about her brothers, her parents' reactions, the war, and being the only one left of the four children, and so she came to talk with me, a counsellor.

The secret mourner

Sometimes a loss is deemed secret and cannot be divulged to those closest around. One thinks here of those who perhaps were the "other woman/man" in an illicit relationship. I am not commenting on the rightness or otherwise of such relationships but on the aspect of grief. How difficult the time of grieving must be for them. They are denied the support afforded by the public acknowledgement of their relationship with the deceased at the funeral. Some may at least attend the funeral but their status there is unrecognized. They may not even be able to talk to any of their colleagues or friends about their loss. Here there is a particular role for the counsellor. It is not for the counsellor to judge but to take the person and their situation as it is, and to be present with them in their time of grief. It may be that the "other party" has not, in fact, died, but simply that the relationship has been ended by one or the other. As with a divorce, this will bring with it a grief reaction but, unlike divorce, it is again secret. I always think that in some ways a divorce or break-up of a relationship is worse than a death because it is man made as opposed to being fate, or God, or nature, or whatever we decide to attribute it to. If the situation is one requiring secrecy it is a more lonely experience and lacks the day-to-day support friends, relatives, and colleagues can afford in the more obvious situations of loss.

There are other situations of loss that are also often seen as very private and that are equally lonely. For example, a girl who has been raped can experience a great sense of loss but will probably not be wanting to tell anyone about the rape. Often in our society people are hesitant to share or talk about some losses, such as the relatives and friends of someone who is lost in a mental illness where they may no longer even recognize their loved ones, or of those suffering from the late stages of Alzheimer's. Relatives are often reluctant to talk openly about what is going on. It is not so uncommon, however, and talking about it could bring support and understanding from others. It could also serve to break down some of the fear and ignorance that often surrounds any kind of disability and illness. Some will recoil, it is true, but at least it means you do not need to guard a secret and perhaps shows you who your real friends are. Is this reticence because of our own fear that we could be next? If you are relaxed in talking about the illness and the problems it entails you can perhaps ease the other person's fear also, so that the relationship and support can continue. It is good that we are beginning to be able to talk more freely about these situations and that there is less of a taboo about mental illness in general. Given that approximately one in four people suffer some kind of mental illness at one time or another it does seem ridiculous to pretend that it does not exist.

Having a baby adopted or having an abortion is often a matter of secrecy, although this applies less nowadays than in the past. In both situations the individuals concerned need to grieve, and they welcome the chance to share their pain in the confidential setting of the counsellor's room. Sometimes a girl may not initially even realize that it is the abortion and the loss that is beneath her depression. It may be that depression or anxiety is the issue she approaches the counsellor with. It is in the work of therapy that it becomes clear that it is the loss of the unborn child that is the real issue. For example, J, whom I referred to in *Short Term Psychodynamic*

Psychotherapy: An Analysis of Key Principles (Rawson, 2002). Here I will give J the pseudonym Jessica.

Jessica came to see me about several issues, but it soon became apparent that the cause of her anxiety and depression was an event that had happened a few years earlier: a termination. Once Jessica had made the connection with her confused feelings and her earlier abortion she was able to come to terms with the loss and get on happily with her life. One of the things she did that enabled her to come to terms with it was to forgive herself. In talking of the termination to the counsellor, an understanding person who did not condemn her, she was able to do this. She also needed to give herself permission to move on, permission to laugh again and to live again. One of the things that helped her to do this was to compose the following poem to the unborn child.

TO OLIVER MARTIN: A gift to you from me

I know I stopped you growing
it's hard to die before you live
but I know you understand
that I had nothing here to give.
I know that I sound selfish
but all I had was love
and even I couldn't give as much
as you have in your world above.
I'll never stop wanting you
or wishing that you're here
but at least I know that you have found a
purer world that's clear.
Don't think I never wanted you
it's just the time was wrong
but I'll love and pray for ever more
at least my whole life long.
So darling as I write this
rest your treasured head

and wish me please some happiness
to replace this awful dread. You know
you'll never be forgotten put down or
mislaid, ignored or just pushed aside coz
here's a pact we made.
I'm going to place you in my heart
a place that's warm and true
and there you'll stay with me on earth until
my soul joins up with you.
I've never really seen the light and beauty that you hold
but chose to see a darker side
deathly black and cold.
But Thomas baby now I see
the pain I have inside
isn't something sinister
but your love I tried to hide.
So will you now believe me
when I say with all my heart
that I love you now and always
and that we'll never part.
One day we'll be together
until then just look and see
that every time I laugh and smile
it's a gift to you from me.

In this beautiful poem Jessica sought the understanding
and forgiveness of her unborn child, she named him, which
is an important step and she perceived him to be in a happy
place. Indeed happier than anything "here below". Also, in
giving "every smile as a gift from me to you", she found a
way of accepting forgiveness and of transforming her former
sadness and guilty feelings into an appropriate gift of love—
that of living and striving to be happy.

Jessica taught me a lot as a counsellor, especially her idea
of "every smile and every laugh a gift from me to you".

Perhaps this idea is one that many who are bereaved could think about. It is at times so hard to pick up the threads of our lives after a loss of a significant other, or to forge the new paths that need to be trodden. The will to do so is so often linked with the one who has gone, but what a wonderful way Jessica's is to help us move forward. To see each happy moment as a gift to the other who has gone before us. Like any other gift, at Christmas or on birthdays, this is not a concept to be for ever harped upon but rather, when needed, to encourage and prod us forward or, from time to time, to remember lovingly. I thank Jessica for this valuable and enlightened idea.

I have described a little of Jessica's therapy work. Was it a successful way forward? Well, in some ways the poem speaks for itself, but in her own words in Jessica's last session—session four—she described it thus: "It was like waking up after a deep sleep."

I have commented that it was in session four, the last session, that she said this, to emphasize that counselling or psychotherapy does not have to take for ever. Often people only need a few sessions—one even—to put them back on track. This is especially so if the problem is one where perhaps something has been repressed or blocked. If the person needs more ongoing support—a kind of checking in—to provide encouragement as they establish new links in the local community, then they might need longer. Here I know that many of my colleagues, who are not believers in the short-term therapy model, may be amazed that I can suggest that a few sessions may be enough. However, my research for a previous book also showed that the average number of sessions for whatever type of issue was between four and six sessions.

It is a fact that some 50% of those attending counselling services within colleges do so for just one session! This was also the case in my own practice within a college. Very, very many of those coming to see the counsellors had issues that were connected with grief. I often found that my role was one of educating the student in the process of grief, in the symptoms and the normality of what they were feeling. They were not going mad!

Grief can block creativity

Jacques, an art student, was referred to me by one of his tutors since he had become aggressive suddenly and seemed utterly unable to produce any art work. The tutor realized that there was a problem but Jacques was very reticent with him and would not open up about his problem. The tutor realized that the lad might speak more freely with someone who was not his tutor, meeting him every day in class, and so brought Jacques to see me in the counselling service.

Jacques was French and was in this country for his course. He could speak and understand English, but this was not his first language. He would barely look at me and I gently suggested that it might help if he talked, since clearly there was something that was bothering him. I explained how talking can help, although there are no magic wands. I mentioned a few of the types of problem people come to a counsellor to talk about. I wondered if language was a difficulty, and if he could understand what I was saying and speak English well enough to tell me what he was concerned about. To all of this I was getting no comment verbally, but Jacques was clearly taking on board what I was saying and generally summing me up. I allowed plenty of silence between each gentle prompting, to allow him space. He was simply unable to speak. The atmosphere in the room though was one of sadness and heaviness. Jacques sat hunched up, head down and looking mostly at the floor, with glances at me when I spoke. After a while I pointed to the paper and felt tips that I always have available and that were on the table between us and asked, "Would it be easier to write it down . . . or draw it? After a little hesitation Jacques took up the pad and began to draw. He chose a black felt tip. A rectangle appeared,then some grass around it, then it was heavily filled in and then came the tombstone. When he had drawn that he put the paper down abruptly and equally suddenly got up and went to stand staring out of the window of my office. All this time he had not spoken and I had remained silent too, attempting to just be with him. Not wanting to break the atmosphere in the room, where I felt that he was reliving his pain and in some silent way allowing me to share it with him, I stayed silent. However, I went to the window and stood beside him, taking the picture he had drawn with me. After more minutes had passed silently I said, "Someone close has died havn't they?" Although there was no verbal reply I understood that I was on the right track. Once again we shared a period of silence. "Can you tell me about it?" I asked quietly.

I eventually gathered that it was his mother who had died suddenly in France very recently. Once he had managed to reveal this the intense "heavy" atmosphere in the room lightened. Jacques then went back to his chair and I returned to mine. This profound silence had lasted for twenty whole minutes. I cannot say what happened to him in that period of time. I do know that I shared a very deep experience within that silence with him, and that it somehow moved him on with his grief. After we sat down again I spoke a little about grief and how many different reactions people have, including confusion, anger, and a loss of creativity, all of which he had been exhibiting in the classroom. I verbalized for him how sad he must be, and the pain he was in, and that it would get better, that his feelings on losing a loved one were normal and not to be frightened of. Our session ended with a much lighter feel. Jacques's hunched-up stance had now become more upright and open, and he was almost able to look at me and even managed a small smile as he went off. We made another appointment to see how things were going.

By the next session he was no longer being aggressive in class and he was back to being able to get on with his creative work again. He had also given me permission to let his tutor know about his loss so there was additional support within the class situation also.

The importance of "being with" the bereaved

The important lesson that I learned there and would like to share with the reader is just how important "presence" is to the one who is bereaved. It is not so much our words that can help but the being there with the person in their loss. So often people say that they don't know what to say, but they do "feel" for and with the person in their loss. This "feeling" and awareness, empathy, and support are tangible, and can be of real help in the person's grief and loss. To stay present in the silence can be a gift any friend or companion can give to the bereaved. Obviously this must be done with sensitivity, speaking or not speaking as appropriate. Sometimes, the friend who simply stays nearby the bereaved, reading a newspaper or quietly getting on with some little job, can be a comfort—there, but not intruding. There, if called upon to share a memory or thought, but not just aimlessly chatting, although a chatterer allows the bereaved either to be distracted for a while or not to have to make an effort at conversations, and this can also be good.

Old grief: loss from long ago

At times people come to see me as counsellor, not having any idea at all as to why they are feeling so down. They are feeling miserable, not able to get on with their life, not being able to shake off a deep gloom. Again they often refer to many of the grief symptoms mentioned above and yet they have not had a recent bereavement. However, as we explore the situation together from a number of different angles it may well be that a bereavement from long ago comes to light.

For example Jennifer came to see me with these symptoms and no immediate reason for them. There had been no loss in her immediate present. I asked, "Is this date significant for you?"

Jennifer replied hesitantly, "Well actually it is the day my daughter would have been eighteen", and she began to cry gently. I asked, "Would you like to tell me about it?"

It transpired that she had come in to see me on the eighteenth anniversary of the day her daughter—who had been terminated—would have been born. When we made this connection together the tears started to flow freely and she realized that this was the cause of her present misery. She told me the circumstances surrounding her termination of all those years ago, what had led to it and her feelings about that, and the boyfriend, and the family circumstances. She had not really shared these painful memories with anyone before and at the time only the professionals who had helped her knew about it. She talked about the loneliness she felt at that time, the guilt and confusion and fear. She had been certain that the baby would have been a little girl. I wondered whether she had named her. It is important for the child to be named and many people in this position do so at the time. Jennifer had not, however, and so we explored the idea of naming her. One of the great difficulties in dealing with terminations can be the namelessness and the lack of any formal place where one can visit as one can with a grave or columbarium. Even when ashes of a loved one are scattered one at least knows where that was effected. There is a physical reference point, and this often makes it easier. There are ways, however, of symbolically creating such a reference point. This will be explored further in Chapter Five .

The loss of a child who might have been is your concern

In the example above it is again the loss of a child who might have been, and again one that had largely been kept a secret. There are a number of such examples and I make no apology for this. Such situations often come into the counselling room for the very reason that people do not like to address them very openly. They come under the secret category referred to earlier. For those of you who perhaps feel that such losses are of no relevance to you, I would like to ask the following question. Could your partner, your wife, your sister, your mother, your friend have had to contend with this kind of loss? Have they had to cope alone because of prejudice, social mores, fear of judgement and reprisals, or stigma? Or because of a certain diffidence in accompanying the person in their loss? If the grieving process is affecting a lady in your life, then it will in some way impact on their behaviour with you. Gentlemen, it is not just a woman's problem; although the sheer physical realities of child-bearing obviously have more impact on the woman, a man has most surely played his part. Men, too, experience loss when a child does not come to term, and need to allow their feelings also. Men can be very upset by this situation but sometimes think that if they show too clearly their own grief at the loss they may make the woman's situation worse. In fact, if all parties were to be honest as to their real feelings on the matter it might help all concerned. Often, in the past, with a still birth or infant death a man might have seen his role as that of dealing with everything as quickly as possible, believing this to be the best way forward. Years ago, neither the mother nor the father in such cases would have been allowed to hold the child, and no name or proper burial place would be allocated. Fortunately, we are now living in more enlightened times, and holding, naming, and a burial service are encouraged. All of these things enable the grieving process to occur and be shared, which helps both the partners and the other children in a family. It is also important to stress that in these situations there are many pressures and expectations. We need to do what is right for us and what is right at the time. If we do this it is then unreasonable to reproach ourselves if later we think we got it wrong. We need to remind ourselves that we did as we thought best at the time.

Our own important dates

In the example of Jennifer, the important date was related to the one who had gone. At times, it is our own special date or event that is the trigger for a wave of loss. For example, the one who is dead not being at the wedding or not being able to share the joy of the new job, promotion, or degree ceremony. This may also apply when one longs for the missing person to be there at times of stress and trouble. Sometimes this then plunges us into a period of grief. The various symptoms have been outlined later in this chapter so I will not preempt them here. It is, however, important to be able to make these links with our loss—and it may have been long ago—or we tend to mislabel the feelings and then they are liable to be given inappropriate treatment.

Having said that, if symptoms that concern you persist it is best to have them checked out. For example, symptoms of panic and lack of breath may in fact relate to fluid on the lung and heart problems, so don't be too quick to leap to the psychological explanation!

Other past losses can be equally upsetting.

It may seem surprising to many that the pain and distress of a past event that happened long ago can be so very present. This is not at all unusual and, indeed, a great deal of the work of the therapist and counsellor is related to the past. Many people have buried events that occurred in the past. Perhaps at the time and at their age they were unable to cope with them and so just blanked the situation out and got on with their lives. For others, they had so many responsibilities that they put their own feelings on hold and that may have been the case for years. Often then, these emotions only get the opportunity to surface when either another shock to the system jolts them into the present, or perhaps the other responsibilities have eased off and now the person has time for themselves the unfinished business floats up and demands attention. At other times, there is just a limit to the emotional material that can be contained and it simply demands to be dealt with. That is not to say that this is where the work of counselling stays. It is important to deal with what counsellors call "unfinished business" from the past, but it is even more important to see how this is affecting the present, to deal with it, and to move on and to get on with one's life.

Common grief reactions

I have already touched on some of the symptoms of grief in the passages above. Some other commonly experienced reactions are listed below. You do not have to experience all or indeed any, although most people will recognize at least some of these. Clearly the nature of the relationship we have with the one who died will influence how we feel about their passing. If we have had little to do with a distant relative or friend, even if at one time of our lives they were of great importance to us, then our reactions are not likely to be very great. A mild sadness and possibly a little guilt or regret that we have repaid them so poorly for what they did for us in the past may be all that we feel. There is a lesson to be learned here, that is, to use the present moment for our signs of gratitude. Waiting can mean that it is too late! Let us learn from that rather than berate ourselves and put the new resolution into practice. If, however, the person was part of our day to day life and maybe we spoke every day, then we are likely to experience much deeper and more significant feelings. They may be fleeting or more enduring. Much of what I write in these pages relates to the loss of a significant other, where the loss is profoundly felt and the emotions are very deep.

Many people translate their depth of loss into the physical. It will be no surprise if some ailments occur at times of grief, especially in the three-month cycles of grief that I say a little more about in Chapter Three. The grief-stricken are also more prone to accidents at this time, since concentration is affected and muscle weakness can also be a symptom. So things get dropped, or snagged, or road accidents occur, or the pan is left on the stove. Special care is needed to compensate for this. Grief is a profound experience and many describe themselves as working on a different level while they are in its throes. Things that were previously of immense importance pale into insignificance in the face of their loss. There is a new sense of priorities and often it proves a life-changing experience.

Mary haltingly tried to describe something of this. "It's as if I'm operating at a much deeper level somehow . . . it's so hard to describe. I'm in pain—an emotional pain and yet I'm aware of being in touch with something very deep and important."

Common grief reactions have been well documented, but how many people are familiar with them? As a counsellor I have enumerated different aspects of this so often. In my view, each person 's reactions vary but there are norms. In their sorrow people may experience the following feelings and conditions.

- Shock
- Numbness
- Severe cold

- Unreality
- Euphoria
- Exhaustion
- Depression
- Sadness
- Sorrow
- Aches and pains
- Seeing/feeling/hearing/smelling the person who has died
- Not feeling anything at all, even pain
- Sleeplessness
- Not wanting "to go on"
- Despair
- Loss of appetite
- Anxiety
- Restlessness
- Inability to concentrate
- Inability to make decisions
- Inability to express yourself
- Inability to be creative
- Churning stomach
- Tearfulness
- Tearlessness
- Guilt
- Relief
- Illness
- Small tasks seeming like mountains
- Time dragging
- Proneness to accidents and dropping things
- Muscle weakness
- Blurred vision
- Nightmares
- Suicidal feelings
- Nothing matters
- A heavy feeling
- Light-headedness

- Freedom
- Needing to go over and over the last days/weeks hours/minutes
- Needing to talk with others, especially those who know what the deceased means to you

This list is not intended to be exhaustive, but rather to reassure you if you notice that you are beset by any of these—they are normal reactions. You may experience some, or none, or all. It is all right and it will pass. When? How long will it take? Well, that is the subject of Chapter Three.

There is one thing that is certain and that is that it hurts! As Mary wrote:

IT HURTS

It HURTS—an almost physical hurt
Yet that it is not—
It HURTS—an all encompassing ache
—a gap—chasm—resounding hollow—
I flail around trying to get a grip
on some tangible point—and flail—and flail some
more.
I grasp at this—and that
and they all fall short.
There's no denying the loss
The grief is solid and real
The loss is now
And the future . . .?
the future looms emptily ahead—meaninglessly distant.

The very finality of death and our helplessness in the face of its inevitability, confronts us with questions and existential issues that perhaps at other times we choose to ignore. Some of these issues are explored in Chapter Four.

So, you're not going mad if you experience any of these feelings after a bereavement. Nor are you "not grieving right" if you do not recognize any of these at all; your way of coping may be different. You might wish to add a new list to the above, it is not exhaustive. For example, I have not mentioned yet the effect on a woman's menstrual cycle. Some women may find that their periods stop for a while and they need to be aware of this so that they can mention their bereavement to any doctor they may attend with reference to their periods. This consideration may alter the doctor's decision as to some of the investigations, etc., that they might otherwise recommend. Others may find that their periods return when in fact they had thought them finished. The woman's cycle can be very affected by a variety of stressors. Some, for example, find that on emigrating the change of scene, climate, the reasons for the decisions to emigrate, all may contribute to the cessation of the menstrual cycle for a while. Someone emigrating and taking up a new life is often in a mourning type of situation, even though they may be "happily" choosing to make this change. It is not good to deny feelings of grief, since if you do they are likely to emerge in physical symptoms instead.

Anticipatory grief

Sometimes there is very little apparent grief after even quite a close death. We often hear people comment at a widower marrying again very soon after his wife has died, perhaps after a long terminal illness. In this sort of situation, much grief work has probably occurred in the months or years of his late wife's illness. This will have gone unnoticed by others who expect a certain type of grieving. Again, do what *you* need to do and let others think what they will!

To some degree middle-aged "children" are prepared for their parents dying, as they see them becoming more frail and increasingly dependent, and experience anticipatory grief to some extent. That is, they begin to reflect upon the fact that their parents are getting older and that they will not live for ever. Life is finite. As they say, "we all suffer from a terminal illness called life" and death comes to us all sooner or later. In our society however, it seems to be more of a taboo than almost any other subject. Yet to talk about it can help. This is especially so in the case of the terminally ill and those people who know that they are dying. Often they long to speak about it with their loved ones and the loved ones long to speak about it to the one dying. Yet both sides refrain from broaching the subject in case it upsets the other and thereby they lose a great source of mutual support and comfort. If you find yourself in such a situation, perhaps it would be good to tentatively enquire as to whether it is all right to talk about it. Each party then has the opportunity of doing so if they wish to. They can always decline, but at least an opportunity is not lost. Such talking provides the opportunity to mend bridges, to complete unfinished business, to tell the person that you love them, or to express gratitude, or to beg forgiveness, and so on. At times there are practicalities that need to be dealt with if one or other marriage partner dies. If the partners had talked a little more before the partner died, it sometimes would have saved the one left much agonizing and heartache. A Will can also be very important and save a great deal of difficulty after a person dies. So many defer making one and so often it is simply left too late.

The loss as a blessing

Yes, there are losses that are seen as a blessing. This might be where someone has clearly been suffering a lot. But the fact that it is a blessing for the deceased still leaves those who were close to them to mourn. There are some deaths, however, which are a real blessing for those left behind.

Take Madeleine, for example. She told me about her father having been burned to death in an accident. One's instinctive response is to be full of concern for her in such a dramatic loss. However, this assumption in her case was wrong. She had hated her father so much, for his violence and abuse to both herself and her mother, that she in no way mourned him. Indeed she was glad that he had gone and that she and the rest of her family could now get on with their own lives without being in constant fear of what might happen next.

So reactions may not be as we, the outsider expect, and I suggest we are all outsiders to another's grief. That includes even members of the same family or friendship circle. Each of us has a particular relationship with another person, so our loss and grief is individual too. So the message to those trying to help is that we need to listen carefully to where the mourner is. To those grieving, be yourself, feel what you feel, and do what you need to do.

John's wife was suffering a long and painful illness. She could do nothing for herself and did not want to live any more, she was ready to die. When her time finally came it was a relief, and although the family missed her and were sad, this was seen as a real blessing for her. Indeed for them-selves, too, since they could not have continued to offer the care and the time her illness was demanding. So the loss was tempered by this reality, but still John had to cope with his new situation: the single life, the loneliness, the shared existence that was no more. Life could never be the same again.

In the next chapter this aspect of loss will be explored more fully.

CHAPTER TWO

It's never the same again

Loss of a partner

Once the loved one is dead, life is never the same again. This applies especially to couples, whether married, co-habiting, or living as "domestic partners", and to children and parents. Those, in other words, whose lives are closely entwined whether practically, emotionally, or both. Although life will never be the same again when one partner dies that is not to say that it will never again be good. Indeed, it could even be better, but for sure it will not be the same. It is this disconcerting fact that contributes to the sense of loss and grief. Yes, of course we miss the person who is no longer there, but we also miss the pattern of life that we had evolved around that loved one. The things we did together, the music we listened to, the places we visited. The time we had our meals, the favourite TV programmes, activities, pastimes. Some of these may have been done or not done in deference to the deceased, so there can also be a sense of pleasure that, as Joan said, "Now I can do this all I want to or when I want to and how I want to".

This is good! Many bereaved feel twinges of guilt at such sentiments, as if it somehow belies their sense of loss for the loved one. It does not. It is simply fact that after, maybe years of compromising, now as a single person in these situations you do not have to and can now do your own thing. Let this freedom to do as you wish be, perhaps, a tiny consolation. It is all right to experience this sense of freedom, and at this painful time you need all the consolation you can get. Do not be surprised when, after a while, friends, neighbours, even family cease to be as solicitous as I hope they were in the early days after your loss. This is normal. It is a pity, but there is a tendency for people to avoid death's consequences. It frightens us and reminds us of our mortality. We know loss hurts and we don't want to be reminded of it. It is the rare friend who will walk the path of grief with us over time and who allows the remembrances, the tears, the confusion, the inability to move on, and the reluctance to begin again.

The poem that follows was written by Mary in the early days of her loss. It points to the struggle and the temptation to opt out, mingled with the glimpses of hope, in the "veiled reality unfolding":

THE LOSS OF A FRIEND

A life before, between, around
the all pervading sound of chirpy cheer and care
and love, though brief but true,
needs must in grief and loss, be found anew.
The absence echoes, echoes--pains and clangs
—the moment lightens, what has been is not lost
—only what might have been. It is not ours to claim.
And yet the past, it is not wholly gone,
the echoes—glimpses—images—imaginings

the known patterns, warmth enveloping,
strengthening in the chill reality of the now.
The now!
Is there some veiled reality unfolding? Glimpsed—
and lost—regained anew
—less brief but present all around.
Draw back the veil
and let realities combine Oh friend of mine.

So how can we begin again?

In a later chapter I look at some of the things people have
found helpful, as they try to pick up their lives once more
and to go on alone. It can be done! At this stage it sometimes
seems almost impossible, but be gentle with yourself and
know that time does heal. Life will be different, you may be
a little different, but the future can be good. I am reminded
of the mythical Phoenix, which is often seen as a symbol of
resurrection. It periodically burns to death but rises again to
new life from its ashes. Often, when a very close loved one
dies, everything seems to go to ashes too. The life and hopes
we had included that person, and when that life is gone a
part of ourselves seems to disappear too.

"A love left homeless / By death forsaken", as Susan
Walter (1998: 40) describes it in her poem "A Silence Loud".
Subsequently, however, over a period of time we re-establish
a way of life without that person, rediscover ourselves,
gather from the past what we choose and discard what we do
not want, and begin again.

Hearts like dented ping-pong balls

Over my many years as a counsellor I found the following
image to be most helpful when trying to find an appropriate
analogy about grief. It is in relation to ping-pong balls.

It seems to me that we are like a dented ping-pong ball when we lose someone we love very much. There is a dent matching the person—all their attributes and characteristics somehow fill that dent—a "Jane-shaped" dent for example. Have you ever eased a dent out of a ping-pong ball in the steam of a kettle? It is an exercise to be done with all due caution so that one does not scald oneself in the process, but it is possible to steam out the dent in this way and although there is a scarred edge remaining in the shape of the original dent, we can once again play ping-pong or table tennis. In the same way I believe that over a period of time the dent in our human hearts gradually fills out and although it bears a scar in the shape, so to speak, of the person who is gone, the heart is back in shape once more. Just as the mended table tennis ball can now sometimes hit the table just on the scar and go quite askew and not at all as planned, so too can we sometimes find that we have a sensitive area that is both stronger and weaker than before.

Many try to fill the dent with other people, which is fine. Some, however, attempt to plug the gap with one other person whom they perceive to be special. There is need for caution here. To return to the ping-pong ball analogy, if we fill in the dent in a ping-pong ball and then also steam it out using the kettle, as time does for us in the case of grief, then as the ball returns to its rounded shape our temporary filling will be ejected. In the same way, if a person more or less fills the gap at a time of loss, it is quite likely that they will, as time goes on, no longer be such a good fit. This is not necessarily the case, of course, because relationships evolve too, but there is a danger that in the early days of loss a bereaved person may be drawn to someone they feel they can lean on, and the other person may particularly enjoy being needed in that way. Once the bereaved partner in the new relationship has regained their emotional strength and innate sense of themselves, each partner may find that the other cannot provide what they need in a more equal, side-by-side relationship.

One needs to be cautious not to move too quickly into a relationship "on the rebound".

Everything is different.

Everything *is* different after a bereavement. The surviving partner finds him or herself in a strange, unfamiliar world of singles. Having inhabited a world of couples for so long, they are unprepared for the difference and probably previously unaware of just how couple-orientated the world is. This is becoming less so as so many divorces take place and more and more people are choosing to set up home alone, but for the newly bereaved this is a strange experience.

Often their former family friends—couples whom they met as a couple—seem no longer to issue invitations. Somehow the single does not fit their pattern. Neither, probably, has the widow or widower already got an established group of single contacts to see more of at this time. He or she will, to a large extent, be starting again. A new relationship is required with the former couple friends because it is different now the bereaved person is single. Often this can prove rewarding since, at times, one or other partner can assume that they are friends because of the partner and now can see that they are wanted for themselves. Sadly, this can also work the other way at times: one no longer has any link or reason to meet with former social acquaintances since they were indeed more friends of the partner than oneself. One needs to start too, to reach out to other single people and enter into new situations.

Even with their children, and other close relatives such as siblings, new ways of relating are required. Again this is usually unexpected, but all of us establish ways of relating to people. Any change in the situation, as there is when a death or loss has occurred, necessitates adjustment. For the widowed, the relationships with the children change, whether they are grown up or not, because each needs to find a new way of relating to the sole remaining parent. The parent too, may feel that they are trying to tackle the roles of both father and mother now, while also grieving. One should not overlook a similar process in the grandparenting role too. Some widows and widowers may have had clearly defined roles within the marriage (for example, one dealing with finances and the other with housekeeping), but in bereavement have to learn the role of the deceased partner. This at a time when they are least able to concentrate and remember things because of their grief. For a parent of young children to now have to cope with all the roles of care giver and provider, when this has previously been shared, is an enormous task. So the bereaved find themselves in an alien world for a while: familiar in some ways, and yet so different.

For the single person who has probably previously had strong links with other singles, to lose one of their close circle is equally devastating. The single person tends to build up a network of friends who are there for them in different ways at different times. Some will be more central to their day to day lives, others seen more rarely perhaps but the bond none the less being strong and a powerful support. The loss of any of these is perhaps more significant for the single person than may be understood by those with partners, where the partner obviously is the primary source of emotional and other support. They too need to find new ways forward, a new "best friend" or new contacts and companionship. The loss of a parent for a single person, even if they have long since left home, may also be more poignant than may be realized by those who have moved away from the primary family into a committed relationship and may well have children of their own. Even if their secondary relationship no longer exists they have still moved on in a different way from the single person, who is not so likely to have children as the widowed and so does not have an inbuilt close family network either.

The disorientation is caused by many kinds of loss

At this point I would like to remind the reader of the comment I made earlier about the many kinds of loss that trigger the bereavement or grief reactions. As I made that observation I was thinking of the many break-ups in relationships and divorce situations, but there are other examples, too.

For people who perhaps have been made redundant there is a similar disorientation. Suddenly they find themselves in a lonely place without the normal programme of activity, purpose, and colleagueship that formerly made up their days. This is a loss, and they can suffer all the symptoms of grief that apply to a death of a significant other. Additionally, there can be feelings of rejection and hurt pride, which do not figure in a death situation, together with possible recriminations and lack of support from a partner. There are the practical losses, too, such as the financial consequences if one is out of work.

Equally, these reactions apply to someone who, perhaps, is going deaf and now finds that they have lost the social interaction that previously they took for granted. They lose the joy of listening to music or having a good telephone contact with friends. They will experience loss and grief. Likewise the person who loses their sight will find him or herself in a new world where former supports do not help in the same way. The same thing can happen in reverse, too. In a recent medical case a blind person who had his sight restored found himself equally disoriented. He now belonged to the "strange" sighted world, and was expected to just get on with his life. His old support networks in the non-sighted world were no longer there for him. He was alone in an alien and frightening world where there was little understanding of his situation since he seemed just like every other sighted person. The sighted simply did not understand his difficulty. Often he could not recognize objects until he felt them and then he could "see" them. He had gained his sight and yet was bereaved in unexpected ways. Those who have lost someone through death also seem, to a casual observer, to be fine but often what is going on beneath the surface is a very different story.

The things that we grieve over can, at times, take us by surprise. It is sometimes only when we lose someone or something that we realise its importance for us. This was the case with Sandra who had been raped as a teenager.

"It'll never be the same again." Years later Sandra was still experiencing grief and anger at the loss of her virginity that had happened in such a violent and abusive way. Something she considered precious and sacred had been stolen from her and there was no retrieving it. She had always expected and planned that the first time she would have sex would be in the act of lovemaking with her husband. She saw her virginity as a special gift to be given to the man she loved.

This might nowadays be perceived as an old-fashioned view. However, it would seem that there are many old-fashioned people still in the world today! Although counselling helped Sandra to deal with the pain, anger, bitterness, and fear about the rape, the sense of sadness at what now could never be remained. This was not in a neurotic sense, but was the simple reality of her circumstances. She was fortunate to find a sensitive boyfriend and eventual marriage partner who helped enormously with the problem of overcoming the sexual difficulties that followed on from the earlier act of violence.

People suffer in their loss

It is important not to underestimate the gravity of the losses described above and the struggles that people go through as they try to come to terms with their particular loss. Sometimes another person's sense of loss makes no sense to those around them. For example, the loss of an animal can be devastating for some. Sometimes this is because the pet has become the person's reason for living. Sometimes it may be that the particular pet was alive when, say, a deceased parent was still alive, and so forms an almost unconscious link with that parent. Therefore, the grief of the pet owner is twofold, both for the pet and for all that the parent meant for them. To the uninitiated, not realizing the link to an earlier loss, such grief over a pet may seem excessive. As a counsellor, perhaps one is in the privileged position of being allowed to see people's pain. How often I have seen people so bravely struggling with their circumstances, who don their smile and façade as they leave my office. To the outside observer they seem fine!

Gradual adjustment

Gradually one becomes accustomed to the changes wrought by loss. The stress of these changes, however, should not be underestimated. The Holmes–Rahe Scale is an inventory of stressors related to key life events and how they impact on health.

The Holmes–Rahe Scale of stressors

Holmes and Rahe (1967) developed a scale of stressors related to life changes. It has been found that the higher the scores on the Holmes–Rahe stress chart (see Tables 1 and 2) the more likely was the subsequent incidence of ill health (McGannon, 1996, pp. 187–188).

The bereaved often find that many of the events and changes shown in Tables 1 and 2 apply to them and, necessarily, many aspects of their day to day living change when their partner dies. Equally this may be the case when a parent dies, or someone who has been a close friend. Hence the stress score at such times is very high. A score of 300 plus

Table 1   The scale of stressors for major life events

Event	Points
Death of a spouse	100
Divorce	73
Marital separation	65
Death of close family member	63
Change in health of a family member	44
Death of a close friend	37

Source: McGannon (1996), based on Holmes & Rahe (1967).

Table 2   The scale of stressors for changes in way of life

Nature of change	Points
Being fired from job	45
Retirement	45
Type of work	36
Living conditions	25
Recreation activities	19
Social activities	19
Sleeping habits	19
Number of family meetings	15
Eating habits	15

Source: See Table 1.

increased the likelihood of the bereaved person developing an illness in the following three-month period to 80%, a score from 150 to 300 equated to a 51% likelihood of an illness developing in the same period, while those with a score of less than 150 were 37% more likely to become ill. The illnesses referred to ranged from a common cold or indigestion, to much more serious illness.

A death has ramifications for all those who knew the person. A widow may find that she has to go to work to support a young family, where before she may have been able to be a housewife and full-time mother. These changes are frighteningly huge and have to be coped with at the same time as grappling with the emotional upheaval caused by grief. Patterns of relating will change. After a loss gradual adjustments are made as one begins to create a new life and to become accustomed to the changes. Gradually too, the emotional turmoil begins to settle and one becomes less conscious of grappling with the effects of grief. The next chapter looks at how long this process can take and the cycles of grief that may be expected.

CHAPTER THREE

How long?

H ow long does it take to come out of grief? This is a question that is often asked. There is no categoric answer but, once again, there are patterns that can be observed. First, it is a gradual process. There is no clear line where one can say on one day "I am grieving" and on the next day, "I am not grieving". Do not be surprised if you still do not feel yourself again for months. A year is often a positive turning point and four years may pass before things really feel more or less normal again. There are no set rules! It is an individual process. However, I have observed a cyclical pattern, outlined below. It may help you to think about this with a diary to hand. Grief can come in waves. It is sparked by many things, as already mentioned, e.g. that special tune, place, restaurant, sporting event, film, or the very ordinary that suddenly takes on a poignancy and the memories return with sadness or, later, possibly with joy. There will be good days and bad days.

Susan Walter (1998, p. 37) wrote the following poem after the death of her husband and with her son dying:

A BAD DAY November 20th 1996

I hate this endless sadness
And the suddenness of the tears;
The battle with the kind of madness
That by denial would lose its fears.
I hate this heaviness of death,
A millstone to the lifting heart;
The tightened throat, the sudden breath,
The grief that takes my world apart.
I hate this separateness from God
That only find the future bleak,
Not knowing if the way I've trod
Will ever bring the quiet I seek.
I hate this shifting patterned mood
That will not even last a day.
That cannot find itself renewed
And takes, from self, the self away.
I hate the need for constant care
That takes from others in their need;
The endless fight to be aware
That by my efforts I succeed.
I hate this hate that skews the mind,
That makes me restless and afraid,
That makes it hard for me to find
That love that is for others made.

As Susan observes, tears come, as and when, they feel like it and anything can trigger them.

For Brian every time he went shopping, for the mundane weekly shop, he found the tears welling up. Each item reminded him of his wife, the whole routine of this activity, pricing the bargains and choosing the treats for the week, highlighted his loss. Shopping had formed part of the companionable routine shared with his late wife, so this very ordinary activity emphasized the gap and how alone he is now.

Brian muses, "Now which joint? . . . a joint for one!? The large tin . . . too big for one? . . ." He abandons the task, departs to where tears can be shed in privacy and takes another step on the path towards acceptance of the fact of the loss, the fact of the changes. These constant little nudges move us towards the next phase of our lives.

The cycles of grief

Over the many years that I have been in the therapy profession I have observed a cyclical pattern to grief. This takes over from the initial reactions, which are as follows.

First reactions

The first reaction to grief is one of shock, a numbness and sense of unreality about the death. There is often anger, frequently quite irrational, at anyone and everything. There is often denial. One observes comments such as, "It can't be. . . . There must be some mistake."

The first seven or so days that, for the majority of people in this country, is often the time that elapses between the death and the funeral, seems to pass with the individual protected a little by this numbness and, sometimes, a sense of being quite dazed. At times like this people often find themselves doing things absentmindedly; for example, starting to walk out of a shop and forgetting to pay. They are not deliberately intending to dodge payment, they are simply not fully "there". Likewise, accidents can happen where, for example, the person simply doesn't notice that they are pouring scalding water on themselves rather than into the cup.

At this time there are the arrangements to make and often the family and friends are rallying around. After the funeral, as family and friends rush back to their work or homes, the bereaved is left alone. The shock and numbness are also beginning to wear off a bit. That is when the worst impact of the loss hits them. They cannot resume the life that went before. Their loved one is gone. This post funeral time seems to occur around day seven or eight after the bereavement. Would this "downer" be earlier where the funeral is virtually the next day, as is the case in some countries? I suspect so, although it may be that it is simply one week after the death that is the significant point. Some cultures seem to recognize this. The Jewish custom, for example, is to have a whole week of set prayers and companionship, with the family gathered at the home of the bereaved.

Three-monthly pattern of grief

After the rituals are over, I have observed a pattern that has a three-month cycle. This cyclical reaction is a zig-zag process; at each three month landmark we go down further but then come up higher, until we finally regain our equilibrium. This is especially marked in the first year but continues to a lesser degree over several years. It is often four years before a loss is fully assimilated, and even then, one should not be surprised if, from time to time, one is caught unawares with a wave of loss. This is perhaps triggered by a tune or comment, a place, or a TV programme, or a film that sparks fond, sad, regretful, or happy memories. In time, it is to be hoped that our "rememberings" will be ones of gratitude for the happy times shared, and the experiences enjoyed, and the lessons learned together.

After the first few days

It seems that after the initial shock, numbness, and sorrow of the first few days there is a gradual coming to terms with the reality of the loss. So there is a very gradual lifting in the mood and the heaviness of the feelings of sadness. However, this takes time and can feel awful!

Grief is like depression but is not

Often this normal process of grieving gets mislabelled as depression. At times antidepressants are prescribed because of this mislabelling. I would stress that grief is normal, does feel terrible, and at times, as Bruce said, "almost as if it is going to consume me". Certainly antidepressants may tide people over for a while but when finally they have weaned themselves, with the doctor's supervision, off the pills, they still have to cope with the grief that has been held at bay by the antidepressants. However, by this time the person may have put in place a structure of a new life and be better able to cope with the feelings of loss that still need to be grappled with. I suggest that such pills might at best be looked at as a temporary expedient if really needed, but I often have found that once people understand the process that they are going through in their grief they are well able to cope with it. They can appreciate it as a normal, but a hard and painful process. Most would prefer to face their grief rather than the possible side effects of many drugs, even if they are not fully aware of what those may be.

To return to the process of grief: after the initial low point subsequent to the funeral and everyone going on their way once more, bereaved people can sometimes feel as if they are wallowing in a depth of emotional pain that only slowly, slowly begins to recede. The weight of grief seems to lighten, little by little, as if one is gradually climbing back towards normality. Piece by piece they begin to gather themselves together and often ploddingly begin to get on with their lives. People often describe this to be "like walking through treacle".

At three months

At the three month point from the date of the bereavement there seems to be a resurgence of the terrible sense of loss of the early days. In some ways, without the initial anaesthetizing numbness that shock provides, this can seem even deeper than the earlier grief. Also, by this time some of the support from friends and relatives has often been withdrawn, since they simply do not realize that it still may be required. At this stage we may have begun to reshape our lives a little and are beginning to get our act together. When suddenly all progress seems to have vanished as we are engulfed by grief once more, the effect of the low seems worse. This low time may last for a few days but then once more comes the gradual climb out of the sorrowful feelings as one continues life.

At six months

At this point another low is hit. The bereaved are struck by this new wave of grief just as they are beginning to feel as if they can see daylight once more. They find themselves, as Jim put it, "back in the black pit of despondency and grief once more, that heavy feeling in the pit of the stomach." This fall takes the grieving person lower than at the three month mark, and again it may last for a few days or just the one, but gradually the feelings begin to make their way up once more and this time reach a higher point than in the previous "down" period.

Then, as Jim said, "I seemed to be climbing up once more, almost imperceptibly, but beginning to feel a little lighter."

At nine months

Jim returned to see me after a gap of some months. He was feeling as if all the progress he had made had disappeared. We looked at the date. We noted that once again it was a three-month multiple since his partner's death, this having occurred nine months before. I explained about this three-monthly cycle of grief that I had observed over my twenty years as a counsellor/therapist and that seemed to be a zig-zag process, the lows being lower each quarter and the highs getting higher subsequently. I suggested that because he was now at the nine-month point his "low" could be related to this cyclical pattern, the good thing being that once again the "up" would be higher than after the six-month "downer". Jim was somewhat reassured by this idea. He had begun to feel that he was falling back and had not been able to make any sense of his sudden onset of sadness and gloom. He could relate to what I was saying and to see this as a natural rhythm of grief was somehow both reassuring and enabling. It made sense of how he was experiencing his grief.

The first anniversary

The date that is the first anniversary marks a real turning point. People anticipate that it may be a difficult time—and it is. One needs to remember that this grief anniversary for someone's death may actually be at slightly different times for each mourner. For example, it may be that a husband was taken to hospital and died there, while the wife was too sick to see him after he went from the family home. So for the wife the "loss" that is observed in the three-month pattern stems from the earlier date—maybe a few weeks even, rather than the date of the actual death. At this anniversary point the depth of sadness, for one or a few days, may be more pronounced than previously and then the weight of grief that has been almost physically tangible begins to lift somewhat. Where it may previously have been a case of putting one foot in front of the other and simply getting through "today", now people begin to feel a little more positive. They start to feel more able to see a future, to pick up those threads of their old life that are still relevant, and to move on into their new life. Of course, in some measure this process has been going on all through the year, but in terms of emotion this really does mark a step forward. Sometimes people are so prepared for the one year effect and have so steeled themselves against a reaction that in fact nothing happens on the day and then they wonder if they are not "normal". Then, when they have, so to speak, relaxed their guard, it can happen that they are hit by a wave of emotion or just a weight of sadness often inappropriately described as depression a few days later. Remember each person's way of grieving is their own; there is no right or wrong so however you react is all right. All I am pointing out here is what does and can happen to many, so that if you experience these reactions you are not taken by surprise.

One year is not the end of the story

Although the first anniversary does mark a significant point in the grieving process, this is not the end of the story. Many people are surprised at how long grief can take to work through; a year does not complete the process. The three-monthly pattern continues into the next year and, indeed, subsequent years, but the troughs are levelling out and the feeling of normality is once again beginning to be familiar.

Fifteen months

Given that the three-monthly cyclical pattern continues into the second year, the next important point is reached at fifteen months, which, notably, seems to herald a further lightening of spirit.

Both Joe and Petra commented, "I caught myself laughing yesterday."

Janice said, "I found myself humming around the house again."

So for them there seemed to be a marked shift in mood. The ups and downs now are perceptibly levelling out. There is very much more sense of acceptance, and the new patterns that make up the fabric of life are seeming more familiar or, in some cases, new adventures are being embarked upon.

The second anniversary

The second anniversary, however, is a landmark that often reawakens the grief but then subsequently seems to mark a new energy and enthusiasm for life. At times the second anniversary is one for which people have not steeled themselves to expect a bad time, as they did for the first one, and then they find that, as Bruce said, "Grief comes and bites you in the back of the neck."This takes them especially by surprise, since they had become conscious of an appreciable amount of progress into their new lives.

How awareness of this three-monthly cycle of grief can help

Being aware of this three-monthly cycle of grief can help us to take the ups and downs more in our stride. In many ways it is akin to women—and those close to them!—becoming familiar with their reactions to their menstrual cycle. Those women who have particular symptoms at that time, for instance, becoming weepy or angry over little things, learn to look at the calendar. In doing so and finding that their period is due they are reassured rather than wondering what on earth is wrong with them as they dissolve in tears over nothing. Their partners, friends, and relatives also can and do learn the pattern, to help to ease interrelationships. In the same way, knowing about the three-monthly cycle of grief can enable us to realize that we are "just grieving" and not " going mad", as so many tend to think when the tears flow or the wave of sadness and sorrow hits. Instead of rushing to the doctor, they rush to the diary or calendar to see how the date relates to their loss. This link can go back years, by the way. Apparent depression can often link with a loss of many, many years ago. For example, the death of a grandparent lost when Janette was just nine years old had not been recognized as causing any problem for her. In fact, the family system had fallen apart at that stage because of the grandparent's role. It was only through looking at the diary and events around the time of year that Janette was feeling so bad that this connection was made. She realized that she had never really grieved for her grandmother. In doing this all these years later she was able to come off the antidepressants that she had been taking for years.

So, as we grapple with the different feelings and emotions engendered by grief we, too, can be reassured as we look at the calendar. As we see the connection with this three month cyclical pattern of grief we can know that it is normal to have a resurgence of the feelings of loss, but we can also know that it will pass and that it will get better. As with women who become more accident prone and liable to catch illnesses at the time of their periods, so those grieving can be more liable to do so at one of the three-monthly points in the cycle of grief. Being more careful at these times and more alert to what is going on emotionally can guard against this. I am not suggesting blocking out feelings, but acknowledging them quite consciously and paying them due attention, so that they do not undermine at an unconscious level.

Not a morbid expectation

Knowing about this cyclical pattern of grief is not intended to set up a morbid expectation of misery as a three month anniversary comes around. It is rather an explanation for what is often an inexplicable gloom that is experienced and that does not seem to fit in with what is happening at the time. If, in looking at the timing in relation to a loss, the feelings seem to fit, the individual usually feels a certain sense of rightness about the connection and experiences relief. Then it can be dealt with appropriately at a conscious level, whether addressed in some way or deliberately acknowledged and put to one side. There are many ideas outlined in Chapter Five as to how to deal with aspects of grief.

It may take four years

Many find that it takes four years before they begin to feel really "normal" again. That is, to feel that they have regained a lightness of spirit and energy that they had formerly. I believe that it is quite usual and normal for the bereaved to take a full four years before they can say to themselves, as Joe did, "I feel more or less back to normal now."

This may surprise some who seem to think that the person should pull themselves together if they are not right as rain after just a few months. An impossible task, may I reassure the bereaved who are so pressured!

Grief does not confine itself to set times

Although I have spent time outlining the three month cyclical pattern that I believe exists, it is good to be aware that grief does not confine itself to these times alone. As previously pointed out, anything can remind us and set off the tears or sad feelings. Do not be surprised at this, it is normal. How often when in a relationship do we think: "Oh I must tell X about this",or "I wonder if Y would like this for lunch", or "Perhaps Z and I could go and see . . .". If we think of the other naturally when they are alive, is it not also natural to continue to so do when they are not. We are creatures of habit. It takes time to realize that we simply cannot relate in the same way any more. There is nothing to stop us turning such moments into warm, loving, grateful thoughts for the one who has gone. In the early days of grief this is likely to focus more on the pain we are feeling at their loss. However, as time goes on we will become more able to remember lovingly without the searing pain.

Force of habit

It is not unusual for us to carry on routinely with activities that we have undertaken over years, but which are no longer appropriate.For example, laying the table for the person who is no longer part of the family circle. They may no longer be there because of a death or it may simply be that there are children who have flown the nest. We are so used to doing things like this on semi autopilot that we should not be surprised or reproach ourselves when this happens. Simply acknowledge the mistake, maybe remember lovingly, or perhaps have a chuckle at yourself, or be grateful for all the happy times you have shared with those who are not there and move on.

> *There is a time to mourn and a time*
> *to leave mourning behind!*

There is a season for everything,
a time for every occupation under heaven.
A time for giving birth, a time for dying,
a time for planting, a time for uprooting what has been
    planted . . .
A time for tears, a time for laughter;
a time for mourning, a time for dancing . . .
a time for embracing, a time to refrain from embracing.
A time for searching, a time for losing;
a time for keeping, a time for throwing away . . .

[Ecclesiastes 3, 1–9]

There comes a time when we either realize that we have, in fact, begun once more to move forward, or perhaps we have to look for ways to pick up the pieces of our lives and move on. There is a danger for some of almost holding on to the pain, since that is the only reality that they now know. In some traditions and cultures there are conventional guide-lines as to when the official mourning is over, or when black should be worn or left off. I think that such customs can be helpful and perhaps we have thrown the baby out with the bathwater, these days, in discarding the old traditions. Now we have to create our own timetables for getting on with our lives after a loss.,There is indeed a time to mourn and a time to leave mourning aside.

As Angela Mann's poem entitled "Wake-up call" suggests:

> Take hold of life,
> reach out in trust,
> unclench, release
> and welcome in the light.
> Too long in shadowed fearfulness,
> stretched taut by chill despair,
> closed in on shuttered self.
> The snows must thaw,
> and sparks ignite
> to fuel creative living.
> Be patient with those small beginnings,
> these early shoots protect from frost
> and notice each new bloom.
>
> [Mann, 2003, p. 12]

Another very lovely poem encouraging us not to give up hope in our loss was chosen by the Queen to be read at the Queen Mother's funeral, but no one seems to have been able to identify the author. It is as follows:

You can shed tears that she is gone
Or you can smile because she has lived
You can close you eyes and pray that she'll come back
Or you can open your eyes and see all she's left.
Your heart can be empty because you can't see her
Or you can be full of the love you shared.
You can turn your back on tomorrow and live yesterday
Or you can be happy for tomorrow because of yesterday.
You can remember her and only that she's gone
Or you can cherish her memory and let it live on.
You can cry and close your mind, be empty and turn your
    back,
Or you can do what she'd want: Smile, open your eyes, love
    and go on.

In Chapters Five and Six I explore how we might indeed "love and go on" and help ourselves and others to cope with their grief. Before this, however, I want to ponder a little on the question that so often vexes us when confronted with death's finality, and that is: what happens after death?

CHAPTER FOUR

What happens after death?

What happens after death? I don't know! We are all familiar with the "near death" stories. We hear of people seeing a bright light, experiencing warmth, and often seeing their loved ones waiting to greet them. Such people report that they were reluctant to come back. They did so, however, since they felt that they had unfinished business here on earth, either for themselves or their families and friends, and somehow felt as if they had a choice. Their experience in this in-between state was not one of fear at all. In fact their experience seems pleasant and what lies beyond attractive and desirable (Kubler-Ross, 1991).

We are also familiar with humorous references to the afterlife, such as the following example, seen in a church newsletter and entitled, "It pays to get e-mail addresses right".

After being nearly snowbound for two weeks last winter, a Seattle man departed for Miami Beach, where he was to meet his wife the next day at the conclusion of her business trip to Minneapolis. They were looking forward to some pleasant weather and a nice time together.

Unfortunately there was some sort of mix up at the boarding gate, and the man was told that he would have to wait for a later flight. He tried to appeal to the supervisor but was told the airline was not reponsible for the problem and it would do no good to complain.

Upon arrival at the hotel the next day, he discovered that Miami Beach was having a heat wave, and its weather was almost as uncomfortably hot as Seattle's had been cold.

The desk clerk gave him a message that his wife would arrive as planned. He could hardly wait to get to the pool to cool off, and quickly sent his wife an e-mail message, but due to his haste he made an error in the address.

His message therefore arrived at the home of an elderly preacher's wife whose even older husband had died the day before.

When the grieving widow opened her e-mail, she took one look at the monitor, let out an anguished scream, and fell to the floor dead. Her family rushed to her room where they saw this message on the screen:

"Dearest Wife, departed yesterday as you know. Just now got checked in. Some confusion at the gate. Appeal was denied. Received confirmation of your arrival tomorrow. Your loving Husband.
P.S. Things are not as we thought. You're going to be surprised how hot it is down here.

In the introduction to the book I said that I would be drawing on the spiritual in looking at death. I forewarned those of you who prefer to avoid such reflections that there would be a section to miss. This is it! You may wish to skip on to the next chapter at this point—or at least to the paragraph near the end of this chapter under the sub-heading "The mystery of eternal life".

A faith perspective

There are many different ideas about what happens after death. For example, the atheist believes that this life is all there is. Christians, on the other hand, believe in an after-life, and that life here on earth is but a preparation for an eternal and happy life hereafter. In some cultures the dead are buried with items such as cooking utensils that are perceived to be of use in the next life. Belief in the after-life is one of the tenets of Islam also. Other religions, some of which I will touch on here, have different beliefs; for example, the concept of reincarnation. Buddhists refer to a "rebirthing" or "rebecoming", and consider that our goal is to reach a stage beyond the cycle of birth, suffering, death, and impermanence. This is a state of contentment called "Nirvana", which can be achieved in this life by a rare few who transcend all cravings, but the majority enjoy this once they have escaped the birth–death cycle in a final Nirvana. The Hindu religion embraces many traditions and beliefs. A core theme, however, is that the ultimate goal is to transcend the life–death cycle and that this can take many lives to attain. Such attainment is termed "liberation" and refers to union with Brahman, the Supreme Spirit, for all eternity. The Jewish religion offers a different view. Judaism sees God as a god of love, justice, and compassion, and creator of the world, and looks for a Messiah to come to establish God's kingdom here on earth. This kingdom would be for everyone, and it is believed that the dead will be resurrected. Some understand this to mean in a physical sense, others see it as a spiritual continuity of the soul (Weller, 1997).

My perspective

Since this book comprises *my* reflections on grief, I write here as a believer in God and, despite the mystery of suffering in the world, I believe in a loving and forgiving God. I am a Christian and a Roman Catholic, and what follows is informed by my faith. There is debate in the counselling world as to how much one should say about oneself and one's own views. Certainly as a counsellor/therapist it is important not to impose one's views and beliefs on the people who come to seek counselling. However, I have found in the counselling of the bereaved that, as the client struggles with the question of what happens when a person dies, I am often asked what I believe. In these instances, although I would always query why the person wants to know and what their own view is first, I will then answer honestly if I think it appropriate. Most of my clients over the years have had no declared faith. They were not sure what they believed at all; some had thought about the question, some had not. They were, therefore, mostly what would be described as agnostics. Or, in other words, "don't knows" as to God's existence, let alone what happens at death. I did not meet one confirmed atheist; that is, someone who believes that there is no God. Where I did decide that it was appropriate to share my belief with those who asked, it seemed to me that as I did so they would hang on to my every word. It was almost as if they were "borrowing" my firm belief and gaining reassurance and hope from this. Well, what do I believe?

What I believe

I think that the essence of a person—that is, what makes that person who they are, which is their soul—lives on; that, after a person dies the essence or soul of that person will continue to exist, and that this existence is one of happiness that will go on for ever. I believe that the person will then know God in a way that is not possible here on earth. Since God is perfect LOVE and is perfect BEAUTY, to be with God in this new existence can be nothing other than perfect. I believe that my loved ones will meet with each other in unity with

God. Where? I do not know where in terms of a place—I do not think it is physical. We speak of heaven, paradise, eternal bliss. But what does this mean? Even colloquially, we refer to a thing being "heavenly", usually meaning that it is simply wonderful or perfect. We hear people returning from holidays saying, " It was like paradise."

Definitions of heaven

When people speak of something being heavenly they mean it was super, lovely, or, as the *Concise Oxford Dictionary* (1991, p. 545) says, "divine", "very pleasing; wonderful". If we then follow through to look up the word divine, its first entry reads: "of, from, or like God or a god . . . and (2) "more than humanly excellent, gifted, or beautiful". Colloquially it means "excellent, delightful" (*ibid.*, p. 342).

We find that the definition of paradise, as another expression for heaven, is as follows: ". . . the ultimate abode of the just . . . A place or state of complete happiness . . . the abode of Adam and Eve in the biblical account of the Creation; the garden of Eden." (*ibid.*, p. 862).

So what about the word bliss? "Bliss" is defined as: "perfect joy or happiness . . . being in heaven", and as a "state of blessedness"(*ibid.*, p. 117).

Blessedness, then, is described as: "happiness" . . . "the enjoyment of divine favour" (*ibid.*, p. 116).

So, in the ordinary everyday language of our time, heaven is perceived to be everything good. It is something to be relished, and desired, and cherished. It is linked with the divine—with God. It is not a place to be feared.

Where do we get these ideas from?

As a Christian one looks to the Bible and in particular the New Testamsent for ideas as to what happens after death.

There are some clues, but clues seem to be all that we are given.

As a child I used to see heaven as a place where there was chocolate in plenty, certainly horses, and kittens, and all the things I loved. I expected there to be beautiful flowers, bird song and, as mentioned previously, any loved ones who had died earlier. I had fully grasped the idea of it being a happy place and interpreted it as I would understand happiness at that time. For someone else, heaven might be seen as having plenty of football, whether to watch or play, or whatever makes them happy. Since I am certain of it being happy I leave it to God to sort out how to balance the multitude of disparate likes so that each and everyone is happy . . . and for all eternity. I'm glad that there is a God to sort out such matters! Now, as I am older, I tend to see heaven as a state of oneness with God, losing oneself and finding oneself in God, being totally absorbed into that "Other" in total happiness. Going out then, from love, in love, and with love to others who reciprocate from their oneness in God, too. A bit like an electric current pulsating to and fro. I think that many glimpse this momentarily in this life.

Divine satellite

Louis Marteau, a therapist and priest, seems to me to be pondering about this idea in his *Theogical Musings*. He wrote this book not so long before he died. In this passage he reflects on television and satellites, timelessness, and unity.

> Television is not the only, or even the most important, of our present day world experiences. The satellites have an even greater impact. By being above the world's surface and reflecting between them we are able to see the whole world, to see the other side of the world as it is happening . . .

Louis reflects how we can now talk to relatives in any part of the world. He observes that he

> can now be with them and talk to them and see them on my computer, with the aid of a little camera. We can truly "be" with one another in a real way. "Being with" is something more than a mere physical presence—it is a state in which our very souls mingle, support, accept and understand all at the same time. It is the whole of me and the whole of them. And now by the wonder of the new science I am able to really be with them even on the other side of the world. This gives me a new musing on the whole concept of prayer, God is the Divine Satellite. With Him and through Him I can "be with" anyone anywhere. But He is not merely outside the world, He is outside time. So I can "be with" anyone at any time—today or in the past,. I can be with the martyrs at the time of their suffering. I can be with anyone anywhere anytime that they can need someone to be "with them".
>
> "Being with" is one of the most important things in life. We can all remember times when the only thing that we wanted was to be with someone. Not to talk, not to have them do something, but simply to need them to be with us. This is true prayer; to be with God. Words and deeds are merely there to help. Being with is the most important element in prayer . . . The satellite has reduced the distance across the globe to an immediacy that had previously been beyond belief. It has broken the bounds of distance. But we are still bound by the limits of time, in the here and now. However the Divine Satellite exists in Eternity. He is not bound by the limits of time. In Him we can be present to Eternity. We can "be with" those who have long since left our boundary of time. We can be with those who in our past have needed our supporting presence as if we had indeed been there at the time. We can "be with" the martyrs at the time of their suffering, we can " be with" those at whose side we were unable to be in our time. Our prayers, our support, is available even here and now. [Marteau, 2001, pp. 25–27]

These musings are comforting. They point to the fact that any regret we might have with regard to the one who has gone can be fixed; it is not too late. Also, if we can be united in this way with those who are gone, then they, too, can be united with us if we call upon them in prayer.

Can we assume the reader knows what Christians believe?

I do not wish to assume that the reader has any idea of what Christianity is all about. I learned to assume nothing from Sally, who was in her early twenties. Sally entered a church for the first time in her life when she attended a funeral of a friend. She was struck by the grandeur of it and the special atmosphere that she experienced there. She felt that there was something special about it. She found the funeral service moving and thought-provoking. She was tangibly aware of something very special there that she did not understand. She loved the words read in the service, finding them poignant, relevant, and hopeful. I was staggered that this was all so new for her.

How to find out

Sally wanted to find out more about God and religion and, despite being a college student, seemed stumped. I asked her how she would find out about anything else that she wanted to know? It seemed as if she did not know how to apply her student research skills (e.g. libraries, internet, books, or relevant people) and common sense to looking into matters of God. I helped to point her towards ways of finding out, such as talking to people she knew to have a faith or to be Christians, perhaps a minister of religion.

I also reminded her how to research in the library and pointed her towards reading the Bible, especially the New Testament, which describes the life of Jesus, or simply to talk to God in her heart. To my surprise she said she would also talk to her Mum, who was a believer and church-goer. It transpired that Mum and Dad had been of the school of thought that likes to leave children free to make up their own minds, so had made no attempt to introduce her to their own faith. I find this approach puzzling, since if one values something surely one wants to share it with others and especially one's children. However, this withholding approach did achieve in Sally an eagerness to know more and at an adult stage when she could look and assess for herself.

When I was a child I thought as a child . . .

So many who have learned of their religion as a child do not perhaps allow it to be developed into an adult understanding as they do with other subjects. They therefore reject what they learned as a child as no longer satisfying their intellect, but fail to look for adult answers to adult questions with regard to religion. To seek to develop knowledge in other areas seems the norm but, inexplicably, in matters of religion this seems more rare. Is it perhaps a hangover from teasing at school or college about being seen to be part of the "God Squad", or a fear of being different, or of being attacked? Over the centuries people have died and suffered for their beliefs—not least the early Christians. Not so very long ago in my grandmother's generation, even here in England jobs were advertised with the rider "No Catholic may apply". Even today it is not uncommon for school children who are known to have and to practise a faith to be attacked. For example, John and James, living in a seemingly civilized Somerset village, are often set upon because they attend a Christian youth group.

So what do Christians believe?

I cite below references to "eternal life" taken from the Jerusalem Bible. In order to put these into a context and, as stated above, as I do not wish to take for granted that people are familiar with the faith that informs the reflections for this book, i.e. Christianity, I outline first, very briefly, what Christianity is about.

Christians believe that Jesus Christ is the Son of God, and that mankind had gone astray from God. To bring the human race back, God sent his son to save us, to show us the way back.

Jesus is understood to be the "Word" of God in human form. Jesus came at a particular point in history from which time our calendar dates, e.g.Anno Domini (AD)—the year of the Lord—and BC (before Christ). The calendar includes Christmas, when He was born into a Jewish family in Bethlehem, Easter, when He rose from the dead, and Pentecost (around our Whitsun holiday) when God sent His Spirit to help his followers after He had gone.

Jesus was seemingly a man like any other and yet . . . ? He lived a life going around doing good. He healed people, He showed people a new way of living, He promised "eternal life" for those who repented of their bad deeds. He told people to "Love one another just as I have loved you" (John, 13: 34).

His words and way of life were seen by the political authorities as a challenge. They felt threatened and sought to be rid of Him. They did this by crucifying Him, which was the way "criminals" were dealt with in those days and in that culture. In fact He was placed between two thieves. Jesus did not condemn his persecutors, but said: "Father forgive them; they do not know what they are doing" (Luke 23: 34).

As He hung on the cross between the two thieves one of the thieves turned to him saying: "Are you not the Christ? Save yourself and us as well."

But the other spoke up and rebuked him, "Have you no fear of God at all?" he said. "You got the same sentence as he did but in our case we deserved it: we are paying for what we did. But this man has done nothing wrong. Jesus", he said, "remember me when you come into your kingdom." "Indeed I promise you"[Jesus] replied, "today you will be with me in paradise" (Luke 23: 39–43).

Minutes later Jesus died. However, this was not the end. We Christians believe that Jesus rose again from the dead. He was seen by his followers and spoke with them and ate with them. Death was not the end.

> he himself stood among them and said to them "Peace be with you . . ." Why are you so agitated, . . . Touch me and see for yourselves; a ghost has no flesh and bones as you can see I have" . . . they still could not believe it, and they stood there dumbfounded; so he said to them "Have you got anything to eat?" And they offered him a piece of grilled fish, which he took and ate before their eyes. [Luke 24: 36–43]

Then he told them "that everything written about me in the Law of Moses, in the Prophets and in the Psalms, has to be fulfilled" (Luke 24 :44).

He reminded them that what had happened was written in the scriptures: "that the Christ would suffer and the third day rise from the dead" (Luke 24: 44–48).

Jesus then sent his followers out to tell the "good news" to others. His followers in time became known as Christians. Jesus ascended to be with his Father in heaven but sent His spirit to help them to "teach spiritual things spiritually" (1 Corinthians 2: 12–13).

Christians believe in life after death—eternal life

I cite below a number of quotations from the New Testament that refer to the after-life, that inform my beliefs, that I think

speak for themselves, and that, not being a theologian, I will
not attempt to explain. Jesus makes many references to "eternal life"; for example, in John 6: 40, John 5: 24, John 3: 15–16,
and He says, "I am the resurrection. If anyone believes in me,
even though he dies he will live, and whoever lives and
believes in me will never die" (John 11: 25–26).

> Jesus offers comfort to his followers, saying:"Do not let your
> hearts be troubled,
> Trust in God still, and trust in me
> There are many rooms in my Father's house; . . .
> I am going to prepare a place for you,
> and after I have gone and prepared you a place,
> I shall return to take you with me,
> so that where I am you may be too . . .
> If you know me, you know my Father too;
> From this moment you know him and have seen him"
>   [John 14: 1–7]

Paul reinforces this and assures us that "no eye has seen and
no ear has heard, no human heart conceived, all that God has
prepared for those who love him" (1 Corinthians 2: 9).

The mystery of eternal life

So where and what is this eternal life? It is a mystery. Will we
have bodies? Well, not material ones as we now know them.
How can we explain this for ourselves or our children?

The Water Bug and the Dragonfly

There is a lovely book on grief that is written for children. It
uses the analogy of the water bug and the dragonfly. In brief,
each of the water bugs observes that one after another the
water bugs climb up a reed, disappear, and never return.
They do not know where they go or why they do not return.
They promise each other that they will come back and tell

each other what is up there, above the water. The next one that goes up finds that after breaking into the surface he is transformed into a beautiful dragonfly. We have all seen the dragonflies with their beautiful shimmering wings and hovering and darting movements catching the light. This particular water bug remembers his promise to go back and tell his water bug friend how lovely it is up here in the sunlight with the lovely flowers, and the variety of green colours in the countryside, and the pleasant breeze. He darts down, but of course cannot penetrate below the water any more because of his transformation. He is no longer able to swim beneath the surface as he could before. So he sighs and goes on his way. They will have to discover for themselves he muses.

It seems to me that this is the way with the after-life. We will be in some way transformed and even if we want to come back we cannot.

Having said that, however, there are ways in which it seems as if people do communicate from beyond the grave— and I am not referring to the use of mediums. As Mary said:

> When my mother and I were sorting out the various papers after my father had died no sooner did we wonder aloud where one important document or another was, than it seemed to be the next piece of paper to surface. On one occasion the appropriate paper even blew onto the table from another desk.

Chance? Maybe. I like to think that somehow those we love who have gone before us can still keep a watching brief over us, though not in any intrusive way. As Theresa, who was dying of cancer, told her son:

> I'll always care for you and be there for you. I'll watch over you but not in an intrusive way. For example I won't intrude on you if you're with your girlfriend, any more than I would in this life.

This was someone who claimed no belief at all in any God, yet she was convinced that she would meet with her brother and aunt, who had died already, when she finally lost her fight with cancer.

Death often makes people ponder about the meaning of life, and about whether there is a God or not?

Similar to seeing someone off at an airport

When we go to an airport with our friends and relatives there are often tears and sadness at the goodbyes. We realize that there will be cheer and joy at their destination as they are greeted and welcomed by other friends and members of the family. This seems a good example of how we might view our journey from life, through death, to what follows. This idea that our friends and relatives will be there to meet us in heaven is commonplace and reassuring for those of us left behind. Our loved ones at least will have company and happiness, even if we, initially, are devastated and bereft.

The finality of death

As we in our grief look death in the face and are confronted with our own mortality, it is a challenge. It causes some to explore the spiritual and this can be a help. For some it can turn them away from God as they rage against him for taking away whoever or whatever it is that they have lost. This is part and parcel of our grappling with grief.

The next chapter outlines a number of ways in which we can help ourselves in our grieving process. The subsequent one also looks at ways that others can help us and we can help others. Both chapters bring together some of the ideas that have been referred to already in the earlier sections, while adding more. I think that it is worth reiterating some points that have been mentioned in earlier sections for ease of reference. It may be helpful to return to these chapters from time to time.

CHAPTER 5

What can I do to help myself?

I n this chapter I want to look at some ideas that people have found helpful and that you may like to bear in mind on your own journey as you grapple with grief.

Be gentle with yourself

The first thing to say is: be gentle with yourself and be patient with yourself. You are in transition, and most people find that change is quite difficult. The status quo, even if not exactly to our liking, is often clung to because it is familiar and therefore comfortable and less effort than grappling with change. Loss, whether of a person or a thing, even of a concept, involves an element of grief that needs to be coped with.

Break tasks down to manageable proportions

If you have much to do that requires concentration break up the tasks into small bits. Even ten minutes at a time with a project will gradually make some inroads into it. Vary paperwork with physical work. For example, reading that report then perhaps walking down to the photocopier, or filling in that form and then making a phone call. Or deal with those bills or the tax return, interspersing the paperwork with hoovering or shopping, going for a walk, or gardening. Confine the task as well as the time allowed for it. For example, in the next ten minutes decide to read just a section and then concentrate just for ten minutes on that section. If it goes well I suggest that you don't just carry on reading, stop as you had promised yourself and have a change. If you don't keep your promise to yourself, you'll find it harder to concentrate for the ten minutes or fifteen that you decide you'll devote to the next time because your unconscious won't believe you and will resist the effort.

If you are overwhelmed with things to do

Try writing a list of all the things that you need to do. If any have a deadline that is imminent, that clearly needs to be tackled first. Decide to spend some time on that one. If all seem equally important, choose the easiest and get that out of the way. Enjoy scrubbing it off the list! Give yourself a reward of some kind for achieving this small step. Aim to complete just one task each day, even if you find you are actually able to progress more than one.

Writing

Writing about your feelings may help. Write as if to your loved one, to a friend, or to your God. Do not fear to write whatever you wish to God—he is big enough to take any anger or negative thoughts that we may wish to hurl at him! He will understand and not in any way hold it against us. Just as any mum would rather her children expressed their anger and hurt than run away and nurse their pain to themselves so, I suggest, it is with God. You may prefer to write to yourself, as if in a diary. Writing is a good way of getting the feelings out of your system and will help you to feel lighter. This does not necessarily happen immediately, since the writing can stir the feelings up, but you may find that this is so later when you have settled down again. It may be that there are things that you wish you had said to the one who has died. Well, say them now, write them down. Equally there may be things you said or did to that person that now you very much regret. So apologize to them, explain how you came to say or do these things. Write out the pain, confusion, anguish, the regret, anger, or resentment, or how you feel in losing them, and of your struggles and difficulties. You can be as open as you like. They will not be hurt now and in the writing you can stop these thoughts from weighing you down, you can release them. Sometimes as you write you will find yourself writing more than you expected and at times what flows from your pen may even surprise you. If you then read over the pages you may see the illogicality in some of what you write. For example: "If only I had done this" or "If only I had not done that", as if the whole course of events would have changed in consequence. It is unlikely!

Sometimes we can be the occasion of hurt to another but not the cause. For example, if I open a door and in so doing inadvertently knock over a precious vase that stands behind it, I am the occasion of its breaking, but the person who placed it in such a vulnerable position is the one who caused the accident. We need to be clear as to our motives. Are these ever clear though? We are so complex at times. Only God can know the innermost thoughts of our hearts. Thankfully He is merciful. It is good to be open about your feelings in this exercise. If you are afraid, having been really open as you write, that the contents of the pages would be damaging to you or others if they were found, then if necessary symbolically and ceremoniously find a safe place and set a match to the writing. Maybe the ashes could then be placed ritually somewhere appropriate. The rubbish bin may be the right place if the sentiments are angry and negative, as a symbol of finality. Or if what has been written is perhaps more loving, forgiving, and positive, it may seem more fitting to scatter them in a favourite place of yours or the other person's. Remember we're all good and bad and the memories can include the bad bits, too, but with forgiveness and regret. It may be appropriate to leave it at that as a final end. Or if you choose to keep that place as a special place, say in the garden, perhaps a particular plant or tree might be planted there too. As it grows and blooms it may be a special reminder. I elaborate on this idea later on. It may be that you want to keep what you have written to be read again at a later date. Do what feels right to you.

I would suggest that if you decide that writing might be helpful you limit the time you spend at it, so that you don't submerge yourself in sad feelings. Maybe arrange the writing session before you have to pick up the children from school, or before your favourite TV programme starts, or before you have to get supper out of the oven.

A goodbye letter

The writing may take the form of a "goodbye letter" to the one gone. A letter expressing love and loss, recalling joyful memories, sad times that were shared and got through, even bad times that were suffered and are now forgiven, resentments that were formed but now have no relevance, that simply impede the way forward unless let go. It might include anger that they have gone—"How could you leave me like this?", said Katy in a goodbye letter she wrote. A goodbye letter can say whatever is in your heart; by writing it down you can get it out of your system and this will help you to close the door on your old life and move on. So many people wish that they had said "I love you" to the one who has gone. Say it now or put it in the letter. What do you then do with it? It could be burned as suggested above, as in this way it allows you to be absolutely free to express the deepest thoughts. The burning itself can be a symbolic end. It could be preserved in a special place. It could be shared with a trusted friend. In some traditions the elder of the group will declare the mourning period over. This can be helpful in marking a turning point. A goodbye letter could serve this purpose also. Our former rituals with regard to when to stop wearing black and when socializing could resume and the grieving period was formally over, also served a useful purpose. As these traditions are no longer commonplace we have to recreate ways to achieve the same psychological end.

"I just want to forget"

Some people will simply want to forget—so any such idea as writing down their feelings would be completely taboo. They want to move on and almost clear out anything that serves to remind then of their old life with the one gone. That is fine. Each one needs to do what is right for them. If it is a case of clearing out, however, it may be that someone in the family would treasure a memento, so it is perhaps worth asking.

If it would help you to get rid of everything and you are unable emotionally or physically to do so, do not hesitate to ask family or friends to help. They will be glad to have something definite to do that they know will help you. It may help them, too. They may be waiting for you to speak out and not want to push you to do this. So honesty can help all round. Also, if perhaps altering a room around or redecorating could help you, then let the ones who could give you some assistance know. If you are moving forward that may serve to relieve them also. Don't just hold back in case they might be too busy or too tired, gently ask. If the first person you ask cannot help, perhaps another person can.

Drawing and painting

Drawing and painting can also help. Don't try to be the world's best artist, simply use pen or paint as a form of word-less expression of emotion. Let the colours express your sadness, anger, or confusion. It helps not to bottle it all up but to release it in whatever way aids you. Even if you've never tried this before give it a go and see how you feel. It can be a surprisingly releasing form of expression and using it may lead to your being able to express anger or sadness and to move through this to hope.

Physical activity

Doing something that takes physical energy can have emotional benefits. Some people take up walking or running —a punch-bag might be good—digging the garden, or wash-ing the car. Whatever helps, do it, and don't worry about what others may think, it is what helps you that matters. Others may simply go back to work and get on with things, and that is all right too. Some will find that they go initially to do this and then go down with flu or a bad cold after a loss. Perhaps in this way they can receive sympathy and maybe support, ostensibly for their physical illness, but also, through this, for their grief.

Remembering symbolically

In an earlier chapter, I touched on the idea of symbolism in helping us forward in our grief. The grave is an important reference point for many people: they visit, they tend the grave, they feel that their loved one is somehow there. It becomes a place where they go to formally remember. This may help them to put aside their grief at other times, and to get on with their lives. For others a different focal point for our "rememberings" is preferred, and in this symbols can help.

Roberta was devastated to find every last photo of her three deceased brothers had been disposed of, together with every other sign of their existence. While this action helped the parents to cope with their loss it was the occasion (not the cause) of great pain for her. She wanted to remember and to have something of her brothers' to comfort her in the loss.

Symbols of remembrance

These may take many forms and depend on the relationship. Some may want to remember a particular quality in the person who has gone, or a particular interest that they may have had. For some a photo is enough. Others want something more or different. A picture could encapsulate what is wanted. Many donate a bench to stand in a favoured place, perhaps in a park. This can have an appropriate inscription.

You can probably think of other ways of marking the life of the one you cared about for yourselves. Such symbols can be useful ways of marking the anniversaries, not just of the day that a person died, but maybe the wedding anniversary, or the birthday, or the day you first met. By deliberately remembering with a symbolic gesture we can sometimes deal better with the wave of grief that can overtake us, particularly in the early days and months of mourning. It will be months probably, too! You may be surprised at how long one is in mourning. It is likely to be a year before you begin to feel yourself again if the loved one was very close to you and if you shared a life with them. Four years is not unusual, as we saw in the chapter entitled "How long?"

Candles

A candle lit at a special time and place can provide a suitable symbol. Many churches have candles available. To light one and remember can be helpful; you do not have to be a member of the church to do this. It can help to do this in a church with all that it can represent in terms of grandeur, or atmosphere, or a sign of another realm, but equally you might choose to do this quite simply at home.

Alice used to light scented candles all over the house on her wedding anniversary, so this favourite aroma became a deliberate and pervasive reminder of her late husband. It reminded her of the good times. As she blew out the candles towards the end of the day it symbolized another end. This time, however, she was in control of the end.

Meggie used a candle in a slightly different way. She lit it as a symbol of life and to remember lovingly the one gone. For her, when she blew it out she was letting go of the loved one and quite consciously freeing herself to get on with her life unencumbered. So many hold on to the deceased, allowing that connection to prevent movement forward. Sometimes it is a sense of loyalty or guilt that makes people do this. For some it seems like a betrayal to go on alone with a formerly shared activity, but it is important to let go in order to be free to move on.

Planting a special plant, bush or tree

Some people find that planting a special tree or bush in the garden can be helpful. This can be chosen to reflect the person; for instance, many roses are called by names that might be appropriate. Or it might be the colour or profusion of flowers that depict the required qualities. Each person will choose something different for their own special way of acknowledging the deceased loved one.

Petra decided to choose a special climbing plant as a symbol of her late husband. She spent a great deal of time choosing the plant, studying the various plant books she had at home. She selected one that for her would always be a happy memory of him in her mind. She wanted it to grow all around the front door of her home in a way surrounding it in his love. She chose a day and time and planted it as an act of love but seeing it also as an ending and a turning point.

The plant had white flowers, which for her was a sign of happiness and new beginnings. The climbing nature of the plant showed the new growth that she was going to allow herself. The name of the plant had meaning for her in relation to the one gone. So it formed a sort of bridge between saying goodbye to the loved one who had died and a welcome to the growth and development of her own life. The whole process formed part of her moving forward in her grieving and beginning again. There is something good about the idea of a living symbol such as the flower or bush or tree referred to above, but there are many other ways too of marking a sad loss.

The following section is not just for women, so those gentlemen who are tempted to skip the next section I would encourage you to read it!

Naming the still-born child, terminations, and miscarriages

As I pointed out earlier, men, too, have feelings about children who might have been. The lost child may be intimately connected with you or it may be affecting a sister, mother, wife or partner, or a child who is close to you. You therefore can help and be helped by being aware of what the woman may be going through. For each individual it is different and only by asking and talking about it can one really know what is happening for the particular person. Ladies, please remember men are affected too.

There were several instances mentioned earlier with regard to a termination or miscarriage where there is no accessible reference point as there is with a burial. It is here that a symbolic reference point can be especially important. In an earlier chapter we saw how Jessica composed a poem to her aborted child. This she ceremoniously read in a beautiful place that she had selected for the occasion. The ceremonial reading was a kind of burial/memorial service. It was a precious moment and served as an end point, as does a burial. The sentiments in the poem would continue and her memories would continue but the poem was a turning point. From here she moved on. It is very important to name a child lost in a stillbirth, miscarriage, or termination. In order to grieve, the existence of the child needs to be acknowledged fully and naming him or her is therefore important. Many do this in their own minds but there is something significant about doing this more publicly. This may be done in many ways and quite simply.

Pippa, who had had a miscarriage and who never referred to her child within her family or amongst her friends, found great relief in the idea of naming him more publicly. She had in her own mind given her deceased child the name James. She decided to mark his birthday down on the calender where all her other important dates were kept. This she did, also marking it RIP. This, needless to say, elicited remarks and questions from the family. For the first time in nine years she was able to talk freely with her husband and other children about the miscarriage and how she felt about it. She discovered that they too remembered and were pleased to be sharing it. To her surprise they welcomed the idea that she had of returning to the place where she had lived at the time. She wanted to go to the cemetery where other members of her family were buried to plant something there in memory of James and to conduct an informal service of remembrance. She found that even her sister and mum and dad wanted to come too, and so they set a date and did it. This emphasizes the point I made in an earlier chapter that such instances of loss are not the prerogative of the woman concerned alone; they also affect the other members of the person's family circle. After the gathering of her family for the simple ceremony she had planned, Pippa told me of the sense of completion and rightness of the occasion. Now the family refer to James quite naturally among themselves, and even with their friends, too. The secret is out and the weight is lifted. There should be no sense of shame in the reality of what has happened, as some have felt in the past. One cannot ignore a miscarriage as if it had never been. The body and mind has prepared itself for new life and has to contend with the loss of that life. We need ceremony and ritual to make this real at times. Such rituals enable the support of family and friends to become apparent also.

The healing power of nature

Nature can provide a sense of peace and healing tranquillity, that requires very little effort on our part, other than getting to it. John, who was trying to support and help a little boy called Baz who had recently lost his father, decided one day to take him out to the countryside. He chose a hilly and open part of the country overlooking acres and acres of a wonderfully varied scene. He took a football too. The two kicked the ball or rested, taking in the countryside scene. For the first time in days Baz laughed and relaxed. Walking in beautiful countryside can be strengthening and restorative. Seeing wild animals and birds and the amazingly beautiful flowers, often appearing in all their individual colours in the most unlikely bits of scrub land, can cheer and encourage.

The seaside with its endless horizon, the sounds of the waves, the space, and the continuity of the tides in this country or the wonderful azure blue of the Mediterranean and the more assured sunshine there, again can prove restorative and revitalizing.

Immersing oneself in the hub of life

In total contrast to the above, it can sometimes be helpful to find a really busy spot where LIFE is going on at its normal pace. Mary found, after the death of her father and the many subsequent weeks she spent coping with the consequences for her invalid mother, that her world for a while shrank to the family home and the atmosphere of loss and sadness. To go back to the city, joining the motorway with its speed and sense of direction into the bright lights, the rush and bustle and purposefulness of ordinary day to day life, was a healthy jolt to the system. Life and activity was going on as normal. She realized that she needed to reconnect with the ongoing norms of day to day life and to help her mother to do so also.

Let them go

Susan Walter's poem, which follows, ponders about whether the deceased too need to be freed by us to move on. I think many may recognize how a loved one almost needs permission to die. Sometimes we see the sick person holding on until the last member of the family has visited. Colleen felt that her mother was so concerned for all her grown-up children that she was clinging to life, but in pain and suffering. She told her how much she loved her and how much all of her children did, but that they were all right and could manage, and that she was free to let go. The mother peacefully died soon after.

Is it the same with those who have gone? Do they need to be freed to go further? Can we hold them back?

LET THEM BE

> If we so miss our dead
> And do not let them die,
> Do we prevent their freedom
> Hold them here, so fearing loss,
> And bind them to our earth's need?
> With hoarded memories
> Do we keep them close,
> Not let the spirit soar,
> And in our comforting
> Imprison them in time?
> They need eternity.
>
> [Walter, 1997, p. 71]

Forgiveness

I wonder whether those who have gone before us need our forgiveness to move to their ultimate destination wherever that might be. Certainly if we harbour bitterness, resentment, or anger about what our deceased have done we will hold ourselves back. We need to let go, to forgive. Even simply saying the words "I forgive you . . .e.g. Mum, Dad . . ." repeatedly, whether silently or out loud can have a good effect on us. Initially it may be simply words, but in time it can become more heartfelt. Often we can learn from others' mistakes. Where they have hurt us we can take steps not to do that to others. There is a school of thought that believes that resentments and anger can have a physical effect upon us, so it is really in our own interests to let go of these if we can. Resentments and clinging on to hurts of the past simply fester, like an unhealed sore, causing pain and debility within the depths of our being. Over time this seems to increase and harden and damages us the more. If we can let this go, in the spirit of forgiveness, it is *we* who are freed and *we* who can then move on. It is we who gain, as in opening our hearts to let go the unforgiven bits, we also are more open to receive love and care from others who could not penetrate the iron doors of resentment.

I'm so sorry

It is often when someone is dying or dead that we wish we could have said "sorry". Often, it is only now that we realize the need to do so. So dead or not, say it to the person. If there is an after-life, as I believe, then they will know. If you do not believe so, but were in their position, would you not forgive someone genuinely being sorry? Learn from your mistakes and move on!

Prayers

For the believer to remember the one who has died, in prayer, especially on anniversary dates, can be most helpful. In some churches there are lists to which people can add their loved one's name. These people are then prayed for by the whole faith community on the next Sunday. In many churches, especially in the month of November, when special prayers are said for the dead, there is often a book or designated place where one can write the name of the person we wish to be prayed for and they will be remembered by the congregation especially throughout that month.

Individual prayer: I love you and thank you

You also may wish to pray on your own, in your heart and mind, for the person or thing that you have lost and the situation you now find yourself in. It can be a way to tell the one who has died that you love them and appreciate all they have done for you. If you are not sure if you believe in a God or

Higher Being don't let that stop you. If there is one they will surely be pleased with your attempts, if there is not, what do you have to lose? Taking time and space to allow your thoughts and feelings to "be" will be of benefit to you.

I have referred earlier to the idea of "being with" another as one of the most precious gifts we can give. Louis Marteau's extract labelled "Divine Satellite" alludes to this also. Being silent with our God, bringing ourselves just as we are, is a wonderful form of prayer that can bring peace and comfort. The words of a folk hymn by Paul Gurr encourage us to do just that.

> Come as you are, that's how I want you,
> Come as you are, feel quite at home,
> close to my heart, loved and forgiven,
> come as you are, why stand alone,
> . . .
> Come as you are . . . just come as you are.

Helping ourselves in the low times

In an earlier chapter I talked about the cyclical nature of grief. Once we are aware of this pattern we can help ourselves through these low cyclical times. We can be extra gentle with ourselves. We can arrange our work schedule, where possible, to be less demanding around that time. We can plan to make a symbolic gesture of respect/remembrance for the loved one, as in the ideas referred to above. Or you could visit their favourite restaurant, playing their favourite tune. You might consider other ways of helping yourself through the bad times, such as the suggestions above, i.e. perhaps painting a picture of your feelings or a favourite scene of the loved one, or looking out the old photos, or cooking their favourite meal as a special remembering exercise. Or perhaps you could treat yourself. Go and have that massage, hair-do, buy the ticket for the football match, go and buy a new suit, or just hang out with mates. Enjoy yourself as you know your late loved one would wish you to do.

Grief is important.

In this day and age we may often not encounter death of someone close to us until we are well into adulthood. This is in contrast to earlier generations when people died much younger and many, for example, died in childbirth, and childhood illnesses were more life threatening. Therefore we are inclined to ignore death and its implications, and it is not a subject that people like to talk about much. Many are afraid of death. Many more are afraid of the death of their own loved ones—anticipatory grief—fearing how they will cope without them. No matter what we think of it, or how hard we try to avoid it, it will one day come to us all and therefore grief will come, to a greater or lesser degree, to all who care about us. It is good that this is so. Would it not be terrible if we could live and die and no one cared. There are sadly some for whom this is so. Most of you who are reading this, however, are doing so because you do care and are suffering loss, or perhaps because you are close to someone who is grieving. Be glad of what you have shared and enjoyed. Even be glad of the grieving. It is one of the most profound experiences of life. It is one that changes us and puts a new perspective on all—at least for a while. Things that seemed important previously may seem quite insignificant in the light of death, and vice versa. Death helps us to see the wood from the trees, what really is important. It makes us question life, and ponder on the mystery of life and death and suffering. Karen Katafiasz (1993, p. 35) writes: "Your grieving is among the most sacred and the most human things you will ever do. It will plummet you into the mystery of life . . . and death . . .and resurrection. Honour it."

It reminds us of our own mortality. It makes us reassess the things we value and how we want to spend our lives.

Be glad of the bad

In every situation and/or relationship there will have been good and bad. At times of loss, often it is just the good that is focused upon. However, looking realistically at the bad can help us. In allowing ourselves to experience the bad things that were within a relationship, be it with a partner, parent, or child, we may experience a whole gamut of feelings. This can apply equally to a former work place or residence, perhaps relating to a redundancy or retirement. The facts are facts. The feelings are real. Our experience of the facts may not be objectively true—an outsider may see a different picture—but subjectively it is true. "Subjectively true" means that that is how it is for us, it is our experience. These feelings need to be allowed expression and various ways of doing that have been referred to elsewhere. To free ourselves we need to forgive the other for whatever we feel aggrieved by as we have touched on above.

So as we recall, for example, arguments, betrayals, let-downs, put-downs, omissions, violence, aggression, drunkenness, neglect, bullying, discrimination, or whatever is our particular difficult memory, let us acknowledge, regret, forgive, and be free. BUT—and it is here where such memories can really help us in our grief—let us be thankful that we no longer need to experience these bad things. Let us see what we have learned from them. How can we avoid inflicting these bad things on others? How can we ensure that we do not allow ourselves to be downtrodden by such circumstances again?

How could we have acted differently to change the former situation? How can we now act differently to avoid a repetition? By that, I do not mean shutting ourselves away and refusing to risk loving or embarking on anything new for fear of being hurt. It can help to remind ourselves that we are all human, we all make mistakes. Often our good intentions and proper attention to what we believe to be right can, for the other person, be experienced as oppressive or unhelpful.

How many children, for example, feel resentful at their parents way of bringing them up? All parents make mistakes but, as Winnicott (1959) says, parenting only has to be "good enough", not perfect!

So be glad in remembering the bad times as well as the good times. First, because you don't have to suffer them any more. That must be a relief, a joy, and consolation in the time of loss where the grief is causing so much pain. You would not be grieving if you did not also love that person. See how we can learn from it also, so that it can help us to grow as persons.

It can help us at times to be more objective about past sufferings by looking at the situation from a different angle. For example, there is a wise saying to the effect that only when you have walked a mile in another's shoes can you understand a little of the kind of person they are or why they act as they do. This understanding may make all the difference as you struggle with the hurt and move towards forgiveness. I am glad that ultimately judgement and mercy are in God's hands alone!

There is another aspect of being glad about the bad. Many people have to be alongside their loved ones as they struggle with illness and a slow disintegration as death approaches. As we grieve and are so much missing the good times and the person themselves, it can help to remind ourselves of the suffering that the deceased was having to contend with. We would surely not wish such suffering on anyone and, short of a miracle, that was the reality of the situation.

Loss can make us aware of our hidden resources

Very many good causes and achievements have been prompted by a death. For example, special crossings or bridges may be built at dangerous road junctions because of a road traffic accident killing a child, this inspiring the parents to campaign, raise money, and prompt the building of the bridge to prevent any other child dying at that same dangerous point.

Christopher Reeves, the actor who is well known for his Superman character, had a riding accident which paralysed him. This has led him to instigate and fund research into similar conditions, which already is producing remarkable results.

Losses can draw from us resources of which we were unaware. They can give us time, which we would not otherwise have had, to be available, perhaps in a different way, for the family or friends. An incapacitating accident, for example, can force us off work and to be more at home. If we do not allow ourselves to turn inwards, but use our presence to listen and be there for others, we may be surprised at how rewarding this can be. It is very special to give time and a listening, interested ear for those with whom we come into contact. Maybe now we have time to write to or phone someone who has been on the pending list for a while!

So how can we begin again?

In trying to pick up the threads of your life it sometimes helps to do the things you did together, to go to the places you went together and to recapture good memories—yes, initially perhaps through the veil of tears. You did these things probably because you enjoyed them too; they will not be the same, but perhaps the intrinsic worth of the place or activity will come through, creating a new spark of interest that may rekindle the enjoyment and perhaps allow it to be seen in a new and different light. Also, by deliberately choosing to revisit these places, you will be less likely to be caught off guard by coming upon them by accident and perhaps then being ambushed by tears and emotion. This will still happen at times, but at least you can take control of some of the occasions in the revisiting schedule.

Getting back to work is often a great help. It has its own routine, structure, company, and pace that carries you along.

However, for those who are unemployed or retired there are less built-in routines and supports. It can then be good to create new routines, pegs to hang the days and weeks on for a while. Perhaps a mundane—even previously scorned—soap on TV can become a comfort in the empty days. Sometimes these same programmes can trigger memories and tears. Does every programme have a death scene, one may begin to wonder? Other memories, too, can be jogged, some sad, some happy.

Re-establishing contact with friends

It is good to stay connected to people, to try to establish new links, and to retain and regain old ones. Re-establishing contact with old friends can help. While you may long for them to be the ones to contact you and suggest "a bite" or "a coffee", don't wait. For, as mentioned before, people often fear to intrude at times of grief and may hesitate, with the best of intentions, to make the first move. Little do they know, unless they have experienced it, just how hard it can be for the bereaved to be the one to make the move. You may hesitate because although today it might seem a good idea, you know that by the time of the date fixed comes you may regret the decision, the effort to socialize seeming just too much. You may, and at times it's good to do so, simply cancel and suggest another day; at other times it's worth the effort and, because it is in your diary, simply to go where the diary directs you. You will, I hope, be supported and regenerated by the contact with a friend. Writing letters to friends can help alleviate the loneliness. It puts us in contact with another and can be an unexpected pleasure these days for the recipient.

Making a phone call to someone can be good too. At times we defer the phone call because we don't want to be committed to journeying to visit and such an invitation might be forthcoming. Just be simple and say so, "Just phoning for a chat since I don't feel like travelling at the moment."

Reaching out to others in their need

It is good to remember that others too may be suffering, perhaps grieving as you are. A quick call, short visit, or a little note can be a great help for them and will probably help you too as you share a little with them and also realize that you are needed, too. Don't underestimate what you can do. Everybody can do something. We are all capable of a smile, a kindly word in the shop or a "good morning" which can make a difference to someone as you go by. You could try asking "How are you?" and really listen to the answer! An offer to child mind, granny mind, sick person mind, to go to the post office, shops, paint or decorate, or fix a broken something can be an enormous help to the other person, and you will gain, too.

Shared memories

It is especially supportive to be with someone who knew the person who has died, since then there can be shared memories and jokes. Yes, it is good to remember the fun times and the funny times and it's all right. Sometimes the bereaved feel bad at the fact that they can have fun again without the loved one, as if it is some kind of betrayal. It is not. Indeed, is it not more of a betrayal to stay in suspended animation and refuse to live? Which of us would expect that of our partner and friend and why should we attribute such ideas to the one who is gone? Unfortunately, at this time of grief some misguidedly do so.

If you are chatting with a really old friend, then you may also begin to recall things that you enjoyed before the loved one existed in your life. It might be good to retry these things again. Maybe the attraction has long since ceased but equally a renewed hobby or work might emerge. It is also sometimes helpful, especially perhaps to the widowed, to remember that they did have a life before being a couple. So often the widowed feel as if they have, as Jim said,"lost half of myself" after such a long time of being a couple. They have to once again shrink back to (or is it expand back to?) being just "one" once more, scarred, it is true, but "one". However, being alone like this after so many years as a couple seems so vastly different, and, again as Jim says, one "just longs for the one who has gone". It might help to remember that, just as there was life as a single person before, so there is life as a single person now. This does not preclude the possibility of once again becoming a couple, but life goes on whether single or not.

A memory book

It can be helpful to gather together a memory booklet for each of the family. Special photos, special recipes, or homely tips. These could be a way of sorting through the photos, cherishing special moments, doing something creative, purposeful, and practical as one looks back and up to the present time. As one hands over the gifts it can also be a symbol of the new start of the next days and weeks for a new collection of memories in the future. As the saying goes: "Today is the first day of the rest of my life". There is a song also that contains the lines "For all that has been. Thanks! / For all that shall be. Yes!"

Old ambitions

It can help to remind oneself of the things one did before, the places one enjoyed and the ambitions one had. Perhaps the latter, if not already fulfilled, may now be given some thought.

New ventures

Now might be the time for improving your qualifications by taking a study course, although for some it might prove a little difficult since concentration can be affected by grief. If this is the case, study or activities requiring concentration need to be undertaken in short bouts, as mentioned earlier, preferably alternating something like reading with something more physically active. The plus factor of taking such a course is that it is a new beginning, its pace is slow, it gives a certain routine, provides contact with other new people, and it gives a direction. It can also be dropped with loss of little other than money and surely some gain in the way of knowledge no matter how far one has gone with it. It may also open doors you would not have considered if the loss had not happened—if only clarifying what you do not want to do!

While I have couched my writing mainly in terms of the loss of a loved one, it is not difficult to see how these same ideas can relate to other situations. For example, loss of job, or even loss of a limb, or loss of home. After all such events what we are attempting to do is to re-establish a cohesive pattern of life once more, one that will at least temporarily hold us together while we gather our resources and rediscover who we are in these new circumstances.

A new hobby can bring us both a lot of fun and contact with new people and also provides a reason to go out and about in pursuit of the hobby.

Who am I now?

As we progress through our grief we need to take stock of who we are, what are our likes and dislikes. If our lives have been entwined with another's much of what we have been doing will be a compromise or merger with the wishes of the other. Now we can choose which bits of this life we wish to take with us into the future. Some bits we will no longer find appealing. Also, what aspects of our own personalities or which of our ambitions or goals did we let go because they did not fit with, say, the family life, or the particular work or place where we were? Now we can choose again. What do I want to do now? What things do I need now? Which things do I not need now? This can be a time of great excitement . . . and, no doubt, some trepidation.

Reclaim the quality you may have invested in the other

Many couples tend to put all of a characteristic into one partner; for example, Dad being the disciplinarian and Mum the softee. Now, if Mum is the one to have predeceased him, Dad can take on the softer role and can reclaim that balance in his life. Another person, who had perhaps allowed the partner to make the decisions, may find enjoyment in the fact that they are now able to make the decisions once more.

The surviving partner of a couple is often heard to say, "I feel as though part of me has been amputated". This can at times leave a different sort of pain. One needs to reclaim that part of oneself that has somehow gone with the departed one. We may be able to name it, as described in the ideas above, but it may be more unspecified. We need all of ourselves as we go on through life, so we need to ask for whatever it is that seems to have gone to come back. We need then to keep hold of it if it seems to want to slip away.

In the case, say, of someone actually losing a limb or a physical ability, it may be important to reclaim some of the other abilities that they possess, ones that depend less heavily on the physical. For example, the musical, or academic, or artistic, or the ability to listen and be there for others.

The loss of a person, or way of life perhaps forced upon one by redundancy, or disability forces us to take stock and re-evaluate what we are about. It tends to bring everything into a new perspective. Health, which we took for granted before, we now realize is of paramount importance. If we lose it, it puts restrictions on us that we have to come to terms with, and to work around if we are not to sink into a pit of despondency. I recall visiting a Lourdes hospital one year and speaking with Angela, a lady whose body was distorted and deformed to a degree where she had to lie on her stomach with her legs bent over her back and her hands to her back also. Everything needed to be done for her in terms of washing, feeding, etc. She remained smiling and cheerful and, despite all, saw life as as good and worthwhile. I was left in awe that she could somehow see beyond her disability to still value the contact she had with others. She even saw value in her disability in that she could inspire others to hope. She appreciated the goodness of the people who cared for her and in her uncomplaining attitude was an example to those of us who get so frustrated when our wants and wishes are thwarted.

"Please go away"

At times the one who has gone seems to be present in some sense. You may find this comforting, reassuring, and helpful, which is fine. It is not unusual. However, sometimes this sense is anything but helpful and is, in fact, distressing. The person, or inner sense, or thought may seem reproachful, as if to say, "How can you betray me like this?" as you are trying to move forward and to get on with life. It is right to say "Go away!" You are living and need to live with the living, not walk with the dead. You are living in the now and not in the past. This in no way negates the part that the deceased person has had in your life, but they are now gone. Neither does it negate your previous way of life and all you have done in it, which will, of course, have influenced where you are now. You have the rest of your life to live as you yourself choose to do.

Unhealthy ways of forgetting

Some are so afraid to face the pain of grief (or the void that is left when one experiences a loss either through death or in another way), that they try to blot it out with drink, drugs, sex, or, a bit less harmfully, excessive work. Excesses in these ways will only multiply the problems. Finances will go awry, friends will be deterred from helping, accommodation can be lost, self-respect can be lost. All can adversely affect the health.

The void will still be there when the alcohol has worn off and more constructive ways of coping need to be found. I hope some of the above ideas may help. There are more, and perhaps the above will spark off some ideas for you.

Counselling

If tempted to opt out through the destructive means mentioned above, then it is good to seek help. Help is available from the doctor, counsellor, friends, pastors, family, colleagues. and bereavement groups.

Counselling or therapy provides a time and place to talk things over with someone trained to listen non-judgementally. It is a place where you can feel free to express your feelings and thoughts in a confidential setting and with someone whom you are not likely to meet socially. Or, if your paths do cross, there is the professional contract of confidentiality to protect you. This process of counselling can provide a necessary support as you go through these difficult times.

It may help you to see things from a different perspective. An example given by Viktor Frankl (1982) describes how he was able to help a bereaved husband who could not see any way through his grief at losing his wife and who was wishing that it was he who had died. Frankl helped him to find meaning in his pain. He pointed out that if it had been he who had gone first then his wife would have been the one to be suffering as he now was. The man had not looked at it from this perspective before and was able from then on to accept his loss, almost as a gift for his wife. This thought helped him as he slowly rebuilt his life as one has to after such a loss.

CHAPTER 6

What can I do to help
the bereaved?

Be aware of what can happen in bereavement

I t can be a great help if you are aware of what a grieving
person can go through, so you yourself may wish to read
up about grief and bereavement, not just the earlier
pages here, but other books also. In this way you may be able
to be more understanding when, perhaps, someone seems to
be irrationally angry for a while, as happens, or keeps dropping things. (You will recall from Chapter Two and the list of
effects of grief that muscles are affected.)

Some of the ideas outlined in Chapter Five could also be
suggested, and perhaps you could work along with the
bereaved with some of the ideas. They may also spark off
other ideas that are more suitable for your friend. My suggestions are just examples.

Don't hesitate to offer help and speak about the loss

At a time of loss it is so hard for the one grieving to make the move, so don't hesitate to make the offer, to issue the invitation. The last thing the bereaved need is to be ignored, abandoned, left to get on with it because we don't know what to say or how to say it. Some cross the road rather than meet the person who has suffered a bereavement. In doing this they exacerbate the bereaved person's sense of loss. Often the bereaved person finds that they are having to reassure others about their own loss. How back to front this is, and yet it is so often the reality.

We certainly need to be tactful, sensitive to what people want and need. We can but ask! Is it so difficult to say, " What would help?", and "I am so sorry", or to give a hug if that is appropriate? If the person simply does not know, can we not try to see if there is some way to help.

As C. S. Lewis says in his wonderful examination of grief *A Grief Observed* (1981), ". . . I want others to be about me. I dread the moments when the house is empty. If only they would talk to one another and not to me."

Often the most helpful thing is for someone to do something practical to help, like the neighbour who brings round a meal ready for eating, or someone helping to prepare sandwiches for the tea after the funeral.

Let them talk

Perhaps one of the most important things is to allow the bereaved to talk about the deceased person and to remember with the bereaved. To remember the good things and the not so good, the funny times, and the serious moments. They existed and their memory lives on, as does their influence on those around them. If the bereaved is moved to tears by this, is that so bad? So many fear to mention the dead person and this can create an unnatural gap. The bereaved need to talk and to go over and over the last moments. A little like a child asks those "why?" questions as a means of learning the language construction as much as genuinely wanting to know why the world is round, or whatever, so do the bereaved repeat again and again the final words or events around the death of their loved one as an attempt to get to grips with the reality, to absorb what has happened, to make it real. They need to do this. They need you to listen.

Cuddles

Very often a hug can express more than many words and often the bereaved is bereft of hugs as their partner, child, or parent is the one who has died. These need to be appropriately given in order not to offend or lead to situations that would take advantage of the bereaved, who are at a vulnerable point in their lives.

A strange new world of singles

I referred in an earlier chapter to the difficulties for the newly single again, in a world in which people are expected to be a couple. You can help here if you know someone in this position as half a couple, a single. If a person has always been single, it is hoped that they will have established a circle of single friends and that this will largely continue. But for the newly single, after very many years of being half of a couple, it is like a foreign country. Very often they find that they are in fact no longer invited to the shared evenings that they used to enjoy with their partner and other couples. Somehow they are perceived as no longer fitting. Or perhaps their friendship was more on the partner's side. Or perhaps one of the other pairs is afraid that their own partner may find the now single bereaved person more attractive and so fears the social gathering on this count. You can help here. It is now, more perhaps than at any other time, that the newly single person needs the support, warmth, and encouragement of their couple friends. I would suggest too, that single people have always needed this also, but that couples do not realize how excluding their couple status can be. At gatherings a couple does not need to make much effort to go out to others, they have each other. The single person has to almost break into this pairing or seek out another lone person. Mostly, I suggest, they fear to try, so remain in their isolation, such being perhaps the greatest sadness of our times. How many elderly folk, for example, when one or other partner has died are exceedingly lonely, and how many younger people also? When marriages or partnerships break down the person who is single again faces this dilemma. Does this then encourage people to rush in to the next relationship, often too soon/ and so the divorce statistics rise once more?

I suspect that, until such time as a formerly married person finds themselves in this position, they will have no idea of this divide between singles and marrieds or those in partnerships. This then can be a real culture shock. They almost have to learn new skills of interdependence and inti-macy in a broader sense than they are used to, where perhaps most of their relating has been to the one other. I am not referring here to a sexual intimacy, but one of sharing thoughts, emotions, ideas, companionship, and comradeship that single people provide for each other. Such comradeship is not, of course, exclusive to singles or to partners. I may seem to be overemphasizing this point, but such is the expe-rience of many who have approached me as a counsellor. Certainly many people could benefit from a greater mix of relationships, couples and singles.

It's not your fault

Children, especially, often need reassuring that the death or the divorce, separation, or accident is not their fault. They can, at times, believe that because they were angry, or had negative thoughts about the people or situations, somehow they have almost magically influenced the events, and so they feel guilty. This feeling sometimes is there for adults too. It can be important for others to reassure them that this is not the case. An accident is an accident and it is *not their fault*. People die when it is time for them to do so, whether you attribute this to God, a Higher Being, fate, or that they have completed what they came for, or whatever particular philosophy you adhere to.

The past needs to be in the past tense

The bereaved often take a while to take in the reality of the loss. They continue to use the present tense in speaking of situations that are past. As Angela said, "Jim and I go walking in the Peak District every year." It can be helpful to gently change the tense for her for example " You must really have enjoyed it when you *used to go* walking—would you like to join us when we go this year?" If the present tense is persisted in, pointing this out to your friend could help them to take another step into acceptance of their loss and the new reality.

Offer to escort the bereaved to a place of their choice.

It can be most helpful to the bereaved to be accompanied somewhere, perhaps to a country spot, where they can experience the ongoingness of nature and absorb some of the healing power of nature referred to in Chapter Five. This applies especially if they are not able to travel alone, or do not feel like doing so. Or it may be that the hustle and bustle of a trip to a busy shopping centre, or airport, or market may be just what is helpful. All of these places can remind the bereaved that life goes on. Even as they are submerged in their grieving ordinary day to day life continues, and they too will become part of the ongoing world once again in due time.

Don't over protect

Dorothy had recently lost her partner suddenly in a road accident. She wondered why it was that none of her colleagues or friends bothered to contact her, whether by phone or by visiting. She felt even more alone, lonely, and rejected. Eventually one of her friends did manage to contact her and told Dorothy how difficult it had been to get past one well-meaning friend. This friend had told everyone she knew to leave Dorothy alone in her grieving. The same friend, who was staying with Dorothy, thus blocked all the attempted calls. She had meant well but had made Dorothy's plight a hundred times worse. Certainly some people might have wanted privacy but ask them, don't presume to know what is wanted. Look and see, offer and ask!

CHAPTER SEVEN

Inching forward in leaps and bounds

W hy this title? As I thought about the way of grief, it seemed to me that often people feel as if they are making no progress at all. As referred to earlier, they often feel that they are walking though treacle. Each step can cost enormous effort, courage, and determination. It often involves an inner struggle to bother at all. So often one hears the question *"What is the point?"*. This applies often, too, for those losing a limb or perhaps suffering a serious change in health that prevents them from continuing the activities that they used to love, or prevents their working any more. It is frequently said by those whose spouse has died that they see no reason to carry on alone, such was the bond of attachment between the two. However as they look back, weeks after a death, they see that progress has been made. For example, everyone has been told, and the funeral has been got through. They have survived those first terrible days. By taking each day at a time, hour by hour they have survived. Months later the headstone has been chosen, ordered, and eventually is in place. This can be a very major hurdle for many and often is not achieved for months, if not years. Often this is a very real milestone, a mark of accepting that the past is past. This may bring with it another flood of grief, which at the time seems as overwhelming and deep as in the first stages. It is more contained, however, and when the tears or wave of sadness passes, one realizes that in the weeks, months, years that have passed, small steps and new beginnings have been made and that one is well on the road to accepting the new world that one now inhabits. As people look back over a year, perhaps on the anniversary, which is one of the big milestones, they realize that although at the time they did not appear to be making progress, in fact they have. Using the step-by-step approach a new skill has been acquired, a hurdle overcome, a new job or hobby acquired, the house redecorated, rearranged, or changed, a new friend has been made, an old acquaintance renewed. A decision has been made as to the next step. They realize that they have a lighter spirit; that awful weight and depth of gloom is dissipated or dissipating.

Gradually those things that had caused sadness, since they were previously shared activities, such as shopping, no longer cause sadness. The special tune, place, programme, memory does not any longer reduce the bereaved to tears or produce that knot in the stomach. They find they are sleeping better, eating better, laughing once more, and enjoying things again.

I hope this might give courage to those who are at an early stage of their grief and I hope it resonates for many who have moved, through time, to this point. There is a phrase that is so often cited to the newly grieving: "time heals". It does, if you let it, trust it! All you have is NOW. If you do what needs to be done NOW, say what needs to be said NOW, you are moving forward and one day will wake up and think: *"This is OK! I'm OK!"*

REFERENCES

Buber, M. (1984). *I and Thou*. R. S. Smith (Trans.). Edinburgh: T & T. Clark.

Frankl, V. (1982). *Man's Search for Meaning: An Introduction to Logotherapy*. London: Hodder & Stoughton.

Holmes, T. H., & Rahe, R. H. (1967). Life change scale. *Journal of Psychosomatic Research, 11*: 213–218.

Katafiasz, K. (1993). *Grief Therapy*. St Meinrad, IN: Abbey Press

Kubler-Ross, E. (1991). *On Life after Death*. Celestial Arts-California.

Lewis, C. S. (1981). *A Grief Observed*. Whitstable: Whitstable Litho..

Mann, A. (2003). *Glimpses of Grace*. Peterborough: Forward Press.

Marteau, L. (2001). *Theological Musings*. London:The Dympna Centre.

McGannon, M. (1996). *Staying Healthy, Fit and Sane in the Business Jungle*. Pitman.

The Jerusalem Bible (1966). Darton, Longman and Todd.

The Reader's Digest Universal Dictionary (1997). London: The Reader's Digest Association Limited.

Rawson, P. (2002). *Short term Psychodynamic Psychotherapy: An Analysis of Key Principles*. London: Karnac.

Walter, S. (1998) *Give Sorrow Words*. Alton: Redemptist Publications.

Weller, P. (Ed.) (1997). *Religions in the UK*. The University of Derby in association with the Interfaith Network for the United Kingdom.

Winnicott, D. W. (1959). *Through Paediatrics to Psychoanalysis*. London: Karnac.

INDEX